ABOUT THIS BOOK

"It is not necessary to change. Survival is not mandatory."
W. EDWARDS DEMING

Why Is This Topic Important?

For organizations to survive and thrive, they must continually change. Effective training is the best way to improve employee knowledge and skill and thus facilitate ongoing behavior change. In 2006, U.S. employers spent more than $129 billion on training. What assurance is there that this sizable investment is yielding a productive training effort?

What Can You Achieve with This Book?

Whether as a student or practitioner in the field, the reader will come away with effective strategies, how-to techniques, and greater understanding of organizational training needs assessment, program design, training delivery, and evaluation methods. *A Practical Guide to Training and Development* provides an overview of the entire training process and the sequence of steps involved to provide effective training.

How Is This Book Organized?

The book is organized in a linear fashion. Chapter 1 introduces the role and competencies of the training professional and the potentially devastating consequences of ineffective training. Chapter 2 focuses on the need to align training with the organization's vision, mission and strategic goals. Chapter 3 reviews methods to identify and prioritize training needs. Chapter 4 reviews ways to design training programs, market them to the organization, and budget appropriately. Chapter 5 discusses training techniques and technology-assisted delivery. Chapter 6 reviews outsourcing as an option for training design and delivery. Chapters 7 and 8 analyze the evaluation process and methods to calculate training's return on investment. Chapter 9 examines ways to promote training's results and ensure continued success.

Note that instructors have the option of accessing an Instructor's Manual, which is posted online at the following URL: www.wiley.com/college/moskowitz

About Pfeiffer

Pfeiffer serves the professional development and hands-on resource needs of training and human resource practitioners and gives them products to do their jobs better. We deliver proven ideas and solutions from experts in HR development and HR management, and we offer effective and customizable tools to improve workplace performance. From novice to seasoned professional, Pfeiffer is the source you can trust to make yourself and your organization more successful.

Essential Knowledge Pfeiffer produces insightful, practical, and comprehensive materials on topics that matter the most to training and HR professionals. Our Essential Knowledge resources translate the expertise of seasoned professionals into practical, how-to guidance on critical workplace issues and problems. These resources are supported by case studies, worksheets, and job aids and are frequently supplemented with CD-ROMs, websites, and other means of making the content easier to read, understand, and use.

Essential Tools Pfeiffer's Essential Tools resources save time and expense by offering proven, ready-to-use materials—including exercises, activities, games, instruments, and assessments—for use during a training or team-learning event. These resources are frequently offered in looseleaf or CD-ROM format to facilitate copying and customization of the material.

Pfeiffer also recognizes the remarkable power of new technologies in expanding the reach and effectiveness of training. While e-hype has often created whizbang solutions in search of a problem, we are dedicated to bringing convenience and enhancements to proven training solutions. All our e-tools comply with rigorous functionality standards. The most appropriate technology wrapped around essential content yields the perfect solution for today's on-the-go trainers and human resource professionals.

Pfeiffer
www.pfeiffer.com
Essential resources for training and HR professionals

A Practical Guide to Training and Development

Assess, Design, Deliver, and Evaluate

Michael Moskowitz

Pfeiffer

A Wiley Imprint
www.pfeiffer.com

Library of Congress Cataloging-in-Publication Data
Moskowitz, Michael, 1952-
    A practical guide to training and development : assess, design, deliver, and evaluate/Michael Moskowitz.
        p.   cm.
    Includes bibliographical references and index.
    ISBN 978-0-470-18946-7 (cloth)
        1. Employees—Training of.   I. Title.
    HF5549.5.T7M676   2008
    658.3'124—dc22   2008012186

ISBN: 978-0-470-18946-7

Acquiring Editor: Matthew Davis   Editor: Rebecca Taff
Director of Development: Kathleen Dolan Davies   Editorial Assistant: Lindsay Morton
Marketing Manager: Brian Grimm   Manufacturing Supervisor: Becky Morgan
Production Editor: Michael Kay

Printed in the United States of America
Printing   10 9 8 7 6 5 4 3 2 1

CONTENTS

ACKNOWLEDGEMENTS

I have had the great pleasure of knowing many wonderful people over the years who gave me opportunities to work with them and for their organizations. I will be forever grateful for their inspiration and for their trust in me.

Dr. Arthur Witkin, Daryl Botten, and especially Susan Roe, Kathy Mandel-Reese, Quelda Wilson, Mary Walshok, Hugo Aguas, Scott Hoganson and Scott Bell, Andrew Salony, Dennis Vincent and Jill Kobrin, David Russian, Kathleen Wheeler, and Bob Zaboronick—each played an integral role in my career. Many thanks to all the business owners, CEOs, COOs, CFOs, CIOs, executive directors, and human resource and training executives who hired me as a consultant to do training and organization development projects for their companies. The best compliment they gave me was to ask me to come back to do more work as well as word of mouth recommendations to their friends and colleagues. The students in my UCSD Extension Training and Development class inspire me every Thursday night.

Judy Loeb put her magnificent editing skills to the test, and Victor Ding applied his amazing analytical talents to this book. Many thanks to my Congregation Beth Am family, who lead me on the path to becoming a whole person each and every day.

Nothing in my life would have been possible without my family. My parents, Martin and Hilda, always told me I could accomplish anything I put my mind to. My sister Raina has been a friend and inspiration to me for as long as I can remember. My kids, Eric and Jessica, are the lights of my life and the best examples of all that is right with the world. And finally, I want to acknowledge my wife Vickie, who is truly my better half and partner in life.

Introduction

"What is training? It is changing behavior."
WILLIAM BRATTON, LOS ANGELES POLICE CHIEF

Training is a critical organizational function. To survive and thrive in today's (and tomorrow's) highly competitive and constantly evolving world, employers must be able to continuously update and improve employee knowledge, skills, attitudes, and behaviors. Effective training facilitates change to achieve organizational goals.

Accomplishing this task with a group of unique human beings is a tremendously difficult challenge. Regardless of whether the training audience is an individual, a work group, a department, a management team, an entire job classification, or the whole organization, achieving success in this undertaking requires meticulous attention and focus on a series of distinct yet interrelated processes. Doing right things right, while not a guarantee for producing desired results, greatly increases chances for a positive outcome. Executing any of the other three possible options—doing right things wrong, wrong things right, or wrong things wrong—ensures a less than optimal outcome.

U.S. organizations spent an estimated $129.6 billion in 2006 on employee training and development, according to the American Society for Training and Development's *2007 State of the Industry Report* (ASTD, 2007). Collectively, they seek to make the best use of this extraordinary investment. Done properly, training is a beautiful win-win proposition for both employer and employee. Everyone loses big time when the effort fails to live up to its promise.

PURPOSE OF THE BOOK

An inscription atop the main branch of the New York City Public Library on Fifth Avenue and 42nd Street recognizes The Astor Library, founded by John Jacob Astor, "for the advancement of useful knowledge." I hope this book makes a contribution to this noble mission.

A Practical Guide to Training and Development bridges the gap between training theory and organizational practice. It also provides an overview of the training function from a linear perspective, describing each of the processes that must be followed in a step-by-step, sequential approach. Scores of practitioners and academic instructors (myself included in both categories) have searched for a book that presents training as it really functions (or should function) in an organization. Many training books are both narrow and deep, focusing in great detail on one particular aspect such as needs assessment, instructional design, classroom delivery, and/or evaluation. There isn't a book that provides an overview describing each aspect of training as one of a continuum of processes that in their entirety constitute the training function. The book is written for this population in response to this need.

Another purpose of this book is to add to the current body of training knowledge by including two original and unpublished research studies, complete with methodology, data analysis, results, conclusion, and discussion. One case study focuses on sexual harassment prevention training and its effect on the trainees' future behavior. A second case study examines the results of 314 completed training needs assessments conducted over a fifteen-year period.

AUDIENCE FOR THE BOOK

A Practical Guide to Training and Development is intended for people in both the academic and organizational environments who wish to achieve greater insight, a better understanding, and the ability to explain the entire training process. Professors, instructors, and teachers, as well as undergraduate and graduate students of degree programs, online universities, adult learners in extension programs for human resource development, training and development, organization development, business administration, and management courses will benefit from reading about the real-life strategies and tools used to execute each phase of the training process. Trainers, human resource professionals, and subject-matter experts who are newly appointed or promoted to positions with responsibility for training in their organizations can model or adapt their practices to the ones described in this book.

SCOPE OF THE BOOK

This book begins by describing the role of the training professional and the competencies that must be acquired and demonstrated to be effective. What follows is a logical, sequential, step-by-step description of the processes that build on one another to create an effective training effort. The book concludes with a discussion of ways to ensure and promote successful organizational training on an ongoing basis. The book includes the following elements:

- Identifying the two essential training elements
- Changing the perception of change
- Understanding organizational change culture: force field analysis
- Identifying training roles
- Developing trainer competencies
- Reviewing the training professional's career challenges
- Effectively train or face the consequences
- Reviewing common training deficiencies
- Strategizing to train effectively for minimized liability
- Understanding vision, mission, and goal alignment
- Conducting needs assessments
- Dealing with resistance to the needs assessment process
- Collecting and analyzing data; using needs assessment results
- Determining training's priorities
- Recognizing the importance of organizational goals
- Overcoming barriers to achieving goals
- Designing programs to engage adult learners
- Strategizing to incorporate adult learning concepts

- Designing a training program plan
- Achieving training goals
- Examining instructor competencies
- Budgeting and marketing strategies
- Choosing and using effective instructional methods
- Assisting training delivery with technology
- Determining internal and external training resources
- Evaluating training impact
- Reviewing technology-assisted evaluation
- Computing training's return on investment
- Examining learning analytics
- Determining marketing strategies
- Establishing an ongoing audit process

HOW THE BOOK IS ORGANIZED

Chapter 1 sets the stage for the rest of the book by defining the role of the training professional and the competencies required to perform effectively. The chapter also examines the change process, and the consequences of ineffective training.

Training must support the organization's vision, mission, and strategic goals, and Chapter 2 explores methods to align training with strategy. The importance of understanding goals is also discussed.

Training should not be designed and conducted until needs are identified, and Chapter 3 describes two different models for determining needs, ranking results, and identifying training topics that will yield the greatest positive impact on the organization's strategic goals. Specific hands-on tools are examined.

After needs are identified and prioritized, Chapter 4 describes how training is designed using adult learning theory to engage trainees and facilitate knowledge, skills, attitudes, and behavioral change. Budgetary and marketing considerations are discussed as well.

Chapter 5 examines the option of using internal or external training resources to deliver training. Effective classroom techniques as well as technology assistance are discussed.

The option of outsourcing training design and delivery is described in Chapter 6. Methods are discussed that describe the best ways to evaluate and determine the best resource fit for the organization.

Chapter 7 reviews a four-tier evaluation process for determining training impact. A fifth tier, return on investment, is discussed in Chapter 8 as well as technological tools that assist evaluation.

Chapter 9 examines methods to publicize training results to the organization. The value of a training audit is discussed as a way to ensure ongoing training success.

How to Use This Book

A Practical Guide to Training and Development contains basic information for those who have limited prior knowledge or experience with training. Consider reviewing all chapters in the order in which they are presented. The chapters present a linear, sequential curriculum that reflects the order that the processes contained within should unfold. I trust you will find what you are looking for.

Introduction to Online Instructor's Manual

The purpose of this manual is to give instructors using *A Practical Guide to Training and Development* as the text for a training and development course some ideas for activities and exercises that can be used in conjunction with the book. Because the book follows the basic flow of training needs assessment and program design, delivery and evaluation, I've found it works well to have learners think through the execution of a training needs assessment (even for a fictitious company) early on in the course and then proceed with the exercises as described in the manual (and the material in each chapter) for subsequent steps in the process. The activities will build on each other as the class progresses, providing a rich and useful experience for all learners. The Instructor's Manual can be accessed through the following URL: www.wiley.com/college/moskowitz

CHAPTER ONE

IN THE BEGINNING

*"We cannot become what we need to be by remaining
what we are."*
MAX DEPREE

PURPOSE

This chapter will enable you to accomplish the following:

- Differentiate between training and development
- Identify the two essential functions of training
- Examine the four distinct elements of the change process
- Review the role of the trainer
- Recognize the consequences of ineffective training

OVERVIEW

A successful training and development effort is more than providing well-received programs for employees—much more. It is built on a philosophical foundation that supports the organization's business strategy. This chapter lays the groundwork for undertaking a comprehensive training and development process. Such a process examines the organization's ability to use training to support its business strategies, goals, vision, and mission, as well as manage barriers to achieving goals. We'll start by defining terms, review the essential elements of training and development, look at the role of the training professional, and finally examine the potentially devastating consequences of ineffective training.

Defining Terms

In the professional literature, the terms training and development are often differentiated. Training usually refers to the activities that help employees do their current jobs more effectively. Development usually refers to the activities that help employees prepare for the next job opportunity. For instance, a Fundamentals of Supervision program would be considered training for a group of new or experienced supervisors. It would be considered a development opportunity for an audience of high-potential non-supervisory personnel.

Identifying the Two Essential Training Elements

Many processes are involved in attempting to accomplish organization-wide initiatives to assist employees in performing their current jobs more effectively and/or prepare them for their next job opportunity. The essence of these processes is composed of two essential training elements.

Change

Ask people for words that they associate with training and development and they will reply with terms such as facilitator, instructor, classroom learning, simulation, policies and procedures, presentation, learning modules, results, feedback, orientation, evaluation, goals, needs assessment, coaching, teaching, interaction, preceptor, instruction manual, computer-based learning, role playing, and so on. These words may appear disparate, but they are all pieces of the processes that people associate with change: learning skills, acquiring knowledge and abilities, modifying attitudes and behaviors, and altering ways of doing business to strengthen job performance. Training and development is a euphemism for change, and change is one of the two essential functions of training.

Goal Focus

The second, equally important function of training relates to what the training and development effort is attempting to change. Training and development, when properly implemented, attempt to facilitate change in employees' knowledge and skill. Knowledge is a set of facts about a subject and the level of understanding that a person achieves through study or experience. Skill is knowledge that a person applies in a particular situation. Enhancing employee knowledge and skill through effective training leads to attitude and behavior change and improved job performance. Overall improvement in employee job performance supports the organization's vision, mission, and goal achievement. In order for the organization's training and development effort to be successful, it must be all about facilitating change that assists the organization achieve its goals. More about this piece of the puzzle in Chapter 2.

Changing the Perception of Change

Ask employees at any organizational level how they feel about change, and many will answer negatively. Words like difficult, unnecessary, unpleasant, uncomfortable, and resistant roll off people's tongues. Employees are generally wary of change. Employees are especially wary if what you are asking them to change (because it is a barrier to goal accomplishment) involves ingrained skills, abilities, behaviors, attitudes, opinions, or ways of doing business. It is a very challenging dynamic. The training and development professional is charged with the goal of facilitating change to improve current and future job performance, often in the face of negative associations with the very concept of change. Moving people from point A to point B when they think they're just fine and dandy at point A is tough. And moving people in a way so they feel good about both the journey and the final destination is both art and science.

William J. Bratton, City of Los Angeles Chief of Police, stated on February 13, 2003: "What is training? It is changing behavior." *A Practical Guide to Training and Development* focuses on the many, many steps the training professional must take to make this change process successful. If there were one simple path or method to achieve this result, the literature would simply say just do this, and employees would magically migrate from one point to another. As one might guess, that is not the case. There is no magic wand or formula to make the right changes happen.

There are certainly ways to help change happen, and there are ways to hinder it from happening, but there are no guarantees. There are, however, definite ways to improve chances for success.

Understanding Organizational Change Culture: Force Field Analysis

Behavioral change can occur through knowledge and skill acquisition in an instructor-led classroom experience, in front of a computer terminal, or in a virtual classroom, but what happens when the attendee goes back to the real world of the organization? Many forces help or hinder knowledge and/or skill acquisition and behavioral change to either flourish or die. Senior and middle managers, supervisors, co-workers, processes, resources, and equipment may help or hinder new behaviors. Force field analysis, a model developed by Kurt Lewin (1947) and reported and adopted by many others, provides a framework for examining variables that influence the change process.

Lewin, a pioneer of social, organizational, and applied psychology, found that in any situation there are both driving and restraining forces to change. Driving forces push or initiate change and sustain it over time. Training combined with managerial encouragement, incentives, and collaborative and/or competitive work group activities, may facilitate change and improve job performance. As a counterbalance, restraining forces act to decrease driving forces. Peer and/or management apathy, hostility, outdated technology, and/or poor equipment maintenance may undo any change in knowledge, skill, attitude, and behavior that training produced. A state of equilibrium, or status quo, exists when the sum of the driving forces equals the sum of the restraining forces. In the training world, a state of equilibrium means no change is apparent. As shown in Figure 1.1, once training is completed and employees return to the workplace, forces abound that will help or hinder implementing and sustaining newly learned attributes.

To sustain training induced changes, one must add or delete driving and restraining forces. The organization's commitment and/or receptivity to change, whether implicit or explicit, is a mirror of its commitment to the training and development effort.

FIGURE 1.1. FORCE FIELD ANALYSIS BEHAVIOR CHANGE AFTER TRAINING

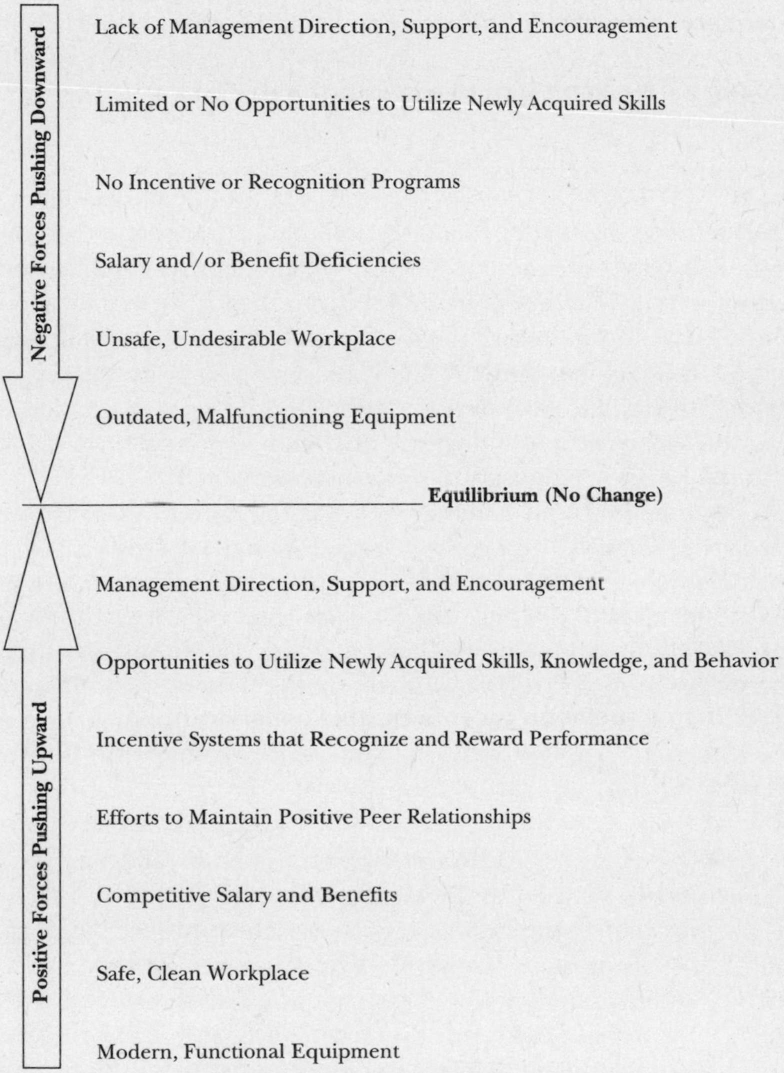

Negative Forces Pushing Downward

Lack of Management Direction, Support, and Encouragement

Limited or No Opportunities to Utilize Newly Acquired Skills

No Incentive or Recognition Programs

Salary and/or Benefit Deficiencies

Unsafe, Undesirable Workplace

Outdated, Malfunctioning Equipment

_____ **Equilibrium (No Change)**

Management Direction, Support, and Encouragement

Opportunities to Utilize Newly Acquired Skills, Knowledge, and Behavior

Incentive Systems that Recognize and Reward Performance

Efforts to Maintain Positive Peer Relationships

Competitive Salary and Benefits

Safe, Clean Workplace

Modern, Functional Equipment

Positive Forces Pushing Upward

The reach of the training and development effort can only go so far. In many organizations, depending on size and resources, there is an OD (or organization development) department that has the responsibility of facilitating cultural (systemic) change by nurturing driving forces and minimizing restraining forces. Ideally, training works hand in hand with OD so the organization embraces change to better fulfill its mission and achieve its strategic goals. According to ASTD's *2007 State of the Industry Report* (ASTD, 2007), organization development received the most resources of any non-training performance improvement solution.

IDENTIFYING THE FOUR STAGES OF CHANGE

A plethora of models describe the change process and the intermediate stages involved in getting from a starting point to an ending point. While these models may use different words to describe each stage along the way, the essential features of many change models are similar. Let's examine four change stages (denial, resistance, exploration, and commitment) from the non-supervisory employee, supervisor and manager, and training professional perspectives using the following example.

Organization A's Customer Service Department has a three-tier hiring interview process. First, a panel of five employees interviews each customer service representative job applicant. Next, two customer service supervisors interview the panel's top three candidates. Finally, the customer service department manager interviews the top candidate. Human resources perceives that the interview process at each tier needs to change.

DENIAL

a. Non-Supervisory Employees. When change was first suggested to the interview panel employees, their overwhelming reaction was to deny that a change was necessary. The employees assumed that the current state, or status quo, was satisfactory, so why change? It didn't matter whether the suggested change was attitudinal ("You need to take this more seriously"), behavioral ("The panel is doing more talking than the candidate"), skill ("Some of the questions you're asking are illegal"), process ("The panel is giving information about the job to the candidate before asking the candidate for job-related background information"), or procedural ("The method the panel is using for evaluating candidates is flawed"). The overriding feeling was: "We don't want to change, and we don't need to change because things are just fine the way they are." The best chance for getting employees past denial is to help them understand the consequences of not changing and to reinforce the perception that the consequences of not changing are more negative than the consequences of changing. In this case, the negative consequence risked by the employee hiring panel is recommending customer service representatives for hire who were not the best qualified candidates in the pool. Additionally, asking illegal interview questions opened the organization to the possibility of a lawsuit.

b. Supervisors and Manager. The supervisors and manager saw the root cause of the problem differently. They thought their interviewing skills were fine. They felt the candidates they selected were willing and able to do the job they were hired to do. They blamed other factors—noncompetitive wages and benefits, outdated technology, equipment and facilities, lack of effective human resource policies and procedures—as the reasons good hires turned bad. They admitted that some hires only minimally met requirements, but they justified these hires as a reaction to pressure from senior management to fill openings as quickly as possible. And after all, as long as they had been conducting interviews they had never been sued for asking illegal questions. So how bad could their interviewing skills be?

c. Training Professional. Feel the plight of the training professional attempting to change the behavior of employees and experienced supervisors and managers in denial about their ineffective interview techniques. Human resources had documented the history of bad hires that resulted in excessive turnover from both voluntary and involuntary terminations after short employment periods; inordinate time had been wasted attempting to resolve employee relations issues; disability and workers' compensation claims had risen; poor productivity occurred because of high absenteeism; and costs had increased from relying on temporary employment agencies.

In this situation, the best chance the training professional has to change the interviewing behavior of employees, supervisors, and the manager is to clearly debunk the myth that the process is fine as is, so it doesn't need to change, making a case for behavioral change by presenting data that exposes the exorbitant costs of excessive turnover in new hires—their rising health claims and poor productivity, the negative effect on the organization's bottom line (money unavailable for pay raises), staffing shortages that contribute to excessive workloads, and lower morale.

Resistance

a. Non-Supervisory Employees. Resistance is different from denial. The resistant employee says/thinks, "I know I need to change, but it is difficult to change. I know I need to change my interviewing technique, but it is hard to because I have been doing it this way for years and I am comfortable doing it this way." Resistance, though, is one step closer to achieving change, because at least the employee acknowledges that change, albeit difficult, is necessary. The best way to help an employee past resistance is to clarify the benefits of the change and to brainstorm (with them) ways to remove the barriers to trying something new. Sometimes, the best way for employees to get past resistance is to suffer the unfortunate consequences of not changing. Recommending the hiring of a co-worker using ineffective interviewing techniques and then experiencing the difficulties working alongside a "bad hire" might be the impetus for changing interview practices.

b. Supervisors and Manager. Consider the circumstances of the customer service supervisors and manager. They are busy dealing with other priorities that significantly impact the Customer Service Department's goals—customer satisfaction and retention, staffing, facilities, and information technology issues. The supervisors and manager know that they are not attending to the process of hiring interviews the best they can but, given their other pressing issues, something has to take lower priority. Finding the time to invest in this process right now is challenging. The supervisors and manager feel they are doing a decent job. If they weren't, they wouldn't have hired and retained any customer service representatives. These supervisors and manager are in a state of resistance about changing their hiring interview behavior and the process they are following; they know they need to change it, but it is hard to do.

c. Training Professional. Again, consider the plight of the training professional attempting to move customer service department employees, supervisors, and the manager past resistance. Explain the benefits of an effective hiring process—for instance, using employees for the hiring panel who take the task seriously and see it as a true developmental opportunity, and training interviewers to (1) conduct effective interviews that get the candidate to do most of the talking, (2) ask legal, job-related questions, and (3) evaluate candidates based on previously established job-related selection criteria—will produce a new hire pool that will turn over less frequently, acquire skills and knowledge more completely, and contribute to reduced staffing issues and better morale.

EXPLORATION

a. Non-Supervisory Employees. After denial and resistance are overcome, exploration is the next step in the change process. The exploring customer service employee says/thinks, "I'll try this change and see how it feels. I'll try doing interviews this new and different way and see how it goes." The best way to help employees embrace exploration is to identify the positive outcomes and benefits of the new behavior. In training jargon, the term is WIIFM (What's in it for me?). WIIFM implies that employees will be more likely to try something new if they clearly envision how the change will benefit them personally. In this case study, a better hiring interview will lead to recommending better customer service representative candidates, which will lead to better hires which will lead to more effective and compatible co-workers.

b. Supervisors and Manager. Consider the circumstances of the customer service supervisors and manager who are willing to explore change. They approach an organizational change initiative with curiosity. They are interested in attempting to implement new interview behaviors and processes for incoming customer service representative candidates. Additionally, their employees will be more likely to understand and accept the rationale behind the request for new behaviors and processes if they see their supervisors and manager doing the same. A powerful message resonates throughout the department when supervisors and manager experience the process and benefits of change together with the other employees.

c. Training Professional. The training professional is in an advantageous position with an audience that is exploring change.

In the case of the customer service department, non-supervisory employees as well as the supervisors and manager will be open to a selection interview training agenda that outlines the structure of an effective interview, delineates legal boundaries, demonstrates open-ended questions designed to elicit maximum information from the candidate, and provides a selection grid to help determine the most qualified interviewees. At the exploration stage, participants are willing, if not yet totally able, to implement a more effective hiring interview. The training program will give them much needed practice, support, and feedback that will more readily translate into new and improved workplace behavior. Employees at the exploration stage are motivated to try.

COMMITMENT

a. Non-Supervisory Employees. Commitment means embracing the change, along with the philosophy of never reverting to former behaviors. This is adopting change at its highest level. The best way to help employees stay committed to change is to continually support and reward their new behaviors. New interviewing behaviors and hiring processes adopted by employees of the customer service department will self-reinforce if they perceive positive results and improvements over previous experiences. But just because employees adopt this level of change doesn't mean they will stay committed. Forces to be discussed later, both personal and organizational, may prevent or sidetrack commitment to change from continuing.

   b. Supervisors and Manager. The supervisors and manager who approach a change initiative with the motivation and energy to make it work will stand a much better chance of making it happen. As with each stage of the change process, a self-fulfilling prophecy is apparent. Their buy-in is swift, their mindset positive, and their determination plentiful. Supervisors and manager committed to change will positively influence those who are less enthusiastic. The best way for a supervisory and manager team to maintain a high commitment level among employees is to model the behavior themselves and mitigate the external factors that impede change from continuing. In the customer service department, commitment to change by supervisors and the department manager will help maintain the new hiring behavior and practices despite the pressure of other department factors (i.e., time crunch to fill open positions more quickly by lowering standards) that may impinge the process.

   c. The Training Professional. Employees, supervisors, and managers at the commitment level of change come to training eager to understand and learn how to behave differently. They know the status quo is not acceptable and are hungry to incorporate new techniques, practices, and processes. If the training program is executed properly, all customer service employees exit with a renewed energy to work cohesively to interview and hire only the best candidates. Time will tell how long they remain committed to this new way of doing business.

Nothing Lasts Forever

Despite one's commitment, changed behavior reverses when the forces of denial and resistance become stronger than the forces of exploration and commitment. We know that people can, for instance, change their leadership behavior, work more effectively as a team, interview differently, stop smoking, or start dieting and exercising—for a period of time. It doesn't necessarily mean the new behavior, any new behavior, lasts forever. Bosses, co-workers, direct reports, family, friends, neighbors, economic conditions, and shifting priorities can all help or hinder changed behavior.

   The goal of facilitating and maintaining positive change in employee knowledge, skill, attitude and behavior over time is a daunting role. It requires the training professional to acquire and use a unique blend of talents to be successful.

Role of the Trainer

Training and development focuses on facilitating change to improve employee job performance. That means the trainer must possess competencies—the skills, knowledge, abilities, attitude, and behavior clusters—to implement specific change required to help organizations achieve their goals. In 2004, The American Society for Training and Development conducted a study titled "Mapping the Future: Shaping New Workplace Learning and Performance Competencies" (Bernthal, Colteryahn, Davis, Naughton, Rothwell, & Wellins, 2004) that attempted to determine a defined set of competencies so that the current and future generations of practitioners provide their organizations with high levels of value and service.

COMPETENCIES

The pyramid model (Figure 1.2) that the ASTD study unveiled includes three layers: (1) foundational competencies including interpersonal, business/management and personal skills; (2) areas of professional expertise including, designing, delivering,

FIGURE 1.2.   THE 2004 ASTD COMPETENCY MODEL

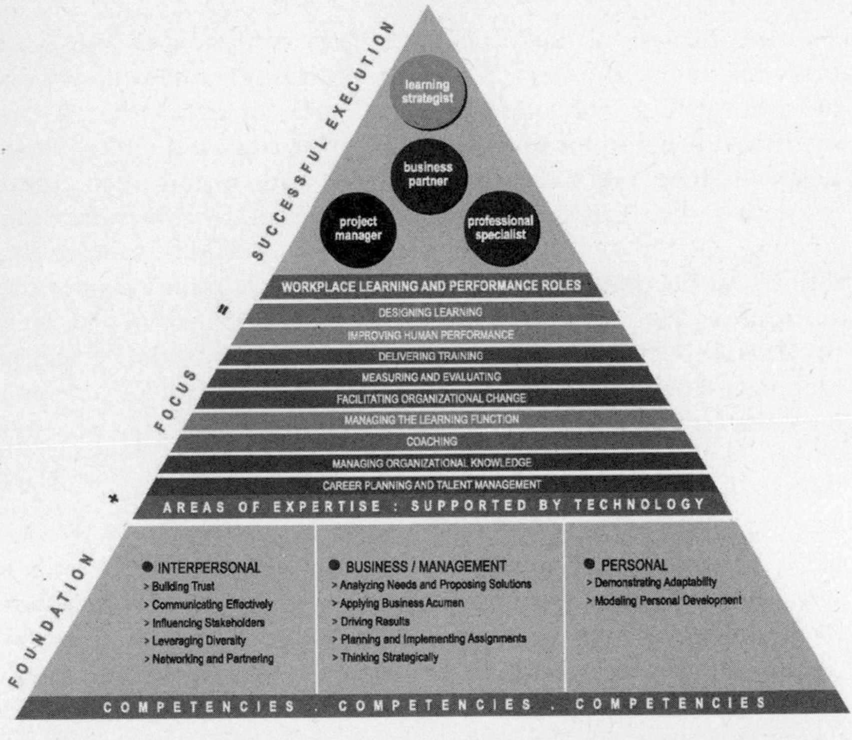

Copyright © American Society for Training & Development, 2004. Used with Permission.

measuring and evaluating training, and (3) organizational roles including those of a learning strategist, project manager and business partner.

Foundational Competencies

Interpersonal skills associated with this competency level include the ability to build trust, communicate effectively, influence stakeholders, appreciate and leverage diverse ideas and insights, and network and partner with internal and external contacts. Business and management skills associated at this competency level include the ability to analyze needs and propose solutions, business acumen, drive results, plan and implement assignments, and think strategically. Personal skills include demonstrating adaptability and modeling personal development.

Areas of Expertise (AOEs)

The second tier of the pyramid include specific technical and professional knowledge and skills areas required for success in the training field. AOEs are specialized areas that focus application of the foundational competencies in specific activities that drive organizational learning and improved job performance. Designing, delivering, measuring, and evaluating training, facilitating organizational change, managing the learning function, coaching, career planning, and talent management are some of the areas of expertise required for successful training professionals. According to the ASTD study, most people in the field spend most of their time designing learning and delivering training.

Roles

The top tier of the model reflects the organizational roles fulfilled by the training professional when effectively applying a select subset of competencies and AOEs. Different roles are often required depending on the project and/or specific situation or need. Like a mechanic reaching into his or her toolbox to deal with a particular situation, the training professionals reach into their vast array of competencies and AOEs to assume the specific role best suited to the circumstance. Learning strategist, business partner, project manager, and professional specialist are each roles that the training person might need to assume depending on current project assignments and organizational needs.

Ultimately, successful training professionals must be able to apply their competencies in ways that support organizational strategies and goals. Chapters 2 and 3 will delve into ways to align training with goals. One overarching training goal is to help employees attain transformational learning in which knowledge converts information into skill enhancement, attitudinal shift, and behavioral change that drives business performance. It is an achievable yet elusive and difficult goal to accomplish. Trainer competencies must be developed in order to fulfill this challenging role. Knowledge of the training topic, good speaking ability, enthusiasm about the topic, focus on training goals, active listening skills, and familiarity with adult learning concepts are some of the competencies that trainers must develop (to be discussed in later chapters) in order to provide a transformational learning experience for trainees.

DEVELOPING TRAINER COMPETENCIES

The 2004 ASTD Competency Study demonstrated that, to be a considered a competent trainer, the aspiring professional needs to acquire a set of skills and knowledge and demonstrate defined abilities and behaviors.

Developing trainer competencies requires much the same process that anyone follows to determine and acquire the knowledge, skills, attitudes, and behaviors needed to work effectively in a chosen profession. The developing trainer must identify the competencies necessary to perform effectively, assess current capabilities, and execute a knowledge and skill development plan to improve their capabilities.

X MARKS THE SPOT; CHECK MARKS THE FUTURE

Quick, take out a pen or pencil and draw a line on a blank piece of paper that represents your training career (this instruction is purposely ambiguous). Now, put an "X" where you are in your career right now. Put check marks where you want to be one, two, three years from now. Getting from where you are today to check marks 1, 2, and 3 requires creating a career development plan. Regardless of one's career choices, it is important to assess the current career state and plot a path for future career development. It is essential to identify the activities that will produce the necessary changes in knowledge, skill, attitude, and behavior to achieve each milestone along the way.

People can expect to average at least three different careers and at least ten different employers in their lifetimes. Whether it's your first or third career, first or tenth employer, assessing current knowledge and skills and planning for improvement is an ongoing process. It doesn't matter whether the current career state is enrollment in undergraduate or graduate school, an after-work evening extension program, or employment for an organization in human resources or some other department. Developing trainer competencies is vital if the career choice is training and development.

Competency-Building Activities

A plethora of competency building activities are available and suggested here in no particular order of importance or priority:

Professional Organizations. The American Society for Training and Development (ASTD), the Society for Human Resource Management (SHRM), the National Training Laboratory (NTL), and the Organization Development Network (ODN) offer courses and various levels of certification for trainers. They also offer individual workshops and seminars in specific competency areas. Attend their annual conferences and local training courses. Join a local chapter and attend its meetings.

Colleges, Universities, and Extension Programs. Public and private colleges and universities, both on an undergraduate and graduate level, offer degree programs that include courses in training and development that teach trainer competency. University extension programs, geared to the working adult learner, also offer certificate courses that include opportunities to develop trainer competencies.

Courses in computer-based learning management as well as training-related graphics or software courses might be available as well.

Internships. Corporations with well-developed training organizations offer internships as developmental opportunities to undergraduate and graduate students as well as high-potential employees who indicate an aptitude and interest in pursuing a training career. These can be excellent opportunities to work alongside trainers and develop competencies in a variety of areas. Consultants and/or consulting firms that specializes in training and development activities also offer such opportunities.

Books, Professional Journals, and Catalogs. Knowledge related to trainer competencies can be acquired by reading and re-reading books (like *A Practical Guide to Training and Development*) and subscribing to and reading articles from professional journals like *T+D, HR Magazine,* and *Training.* It's also a great way to stay current on the latest developments in the field as well as reviewing catalogs of training-related instruments, games, and computer-assisted learning tools.

Websites. Continually browse training-related websites for the latest trends, research studies and recent publications in the field. Using search engines (such as Google or Yahoo) to find specific training-related topics, organizations, materials, and research will help educate the training professional and further develop competencies.

Mentors. Establish mentor/coaching relationships with other training and development professionals in the community who are willing and able to share their time and expertise with new or aspiring trainers. Mentor relationships can be formal (internships) or informal. Mentors and coaches can provide insight into the training role, challenges faced, and different methods used in the field.

Product Vendors. Contact vendors that sell and/or support training materials and receive training on their products and services. Product vendors are usually very knowledgeable about the products and services they provide. Aspiring training professionals can perhaps, in the future, apply the expertise they gain toward a professional opportunity they are pursuing.

Training Vendors. Training vendors like the American Management Association (AMA) and the Center for Creative Leadership (CCL) offer trainer competency development programs, seminars and workshops. Organizations like Toastmasters focus on improving public speaking and platform skills and abilities, essential competencies for training professionals.

Volunteer. Volunteer to use trainer competencies (assess training needs, design and conduct, and evaluate programs) for organizations that cannot afford to pay for the expertise. The practice of using knowledge and skills related to these processes will be an invaluable experience for the fledging training professional when they are called on to perform similar responsibilities in the future.

Observe and Take Note. As a participant in training programs, observe the competencies of the trainer(s) leading the session(s) and note the abilities and behaviors that they demonstrate. Conversely, note whatever detracts from the learning experience. Plan to model the positive abilities and behaviors that you observed when you are the one standing and delivering in front of the classroom.

Observations and Notes from Trainees. One of the wonders of an instructor-led classroom experience is that each trainee observes and learns something different, even though everyone in the room is part of the same presentation. This seems to be a reoccurring phenomenon, as trainees typically internalize different elements of a training experience in individual ways, depending on their previous experiences and knowledge.

Recently, trainees in an overview course on training and development were required to design and conduct a short training program. At the class' conclusion, they were asked to write a key learning they would take away from their training experience. Each answer was different, some more profound than others. Yet they revealed a knowledge and/or skill and/or behavioral change that would enhance their ability and competency to perform as a training professional in the future. Their verbatim comments included the following:

- "It is important to be sure that the room/conference room is set up properly before beginning the presentation."
- "Prepare thoroughly and do not add unplanned items to the training program."
- "Keep people energized. Overall, I think keeping people interested will increase the overall experience and how much they take away from the training."

- "Use PowerPoint as a tool but not as a script."
- "Narrowing and focusing the content to fit the timeframe is very important. It's tricky when the scope of the training topic is very broad."
- "I'll remember how important it is to involve the audience even by doing simple things like asking them questions."
- "Know your audience and who to look at."
- "Creativity and enthusiasm are key ingredients in making a presentation successful."
- "Training is a lot more work than I imagined. Remembering everything to do to make it a successful experience for the trainees is challenging."
- "Training is not as hard as I thought it would be. Practice makes it achievable."
- "It was a great experience to actually stand in front of an audience and deliver a training program. Keep the content simple and it will be easier for the trainer and the audience to get the message."
- "Be comfortable with silence when you ask the audience a question and no one answers right away."
- "I need to slow down when presenting."
- "I am not good at training when I am not fully knowledgeable and comfortable with the topic. I am not good at faking it."
- "Never assume that the audience doesn't have questions."
- "I learned that standing in front of an audience is very hard for me but I did it!"
- "Practice makes perfect."

Common Themes. The common theme of these comments is that, regardless of the specific insight gained, participation in a developmental training activity appeared to have a positive effect on the trainee's perception of their competency. It is unclear whether trainees will take their new-found insight and apply it to a training opportunity in their workplace (a self/peer reported follow-up of behavioral change would add an interesting evaluation piece to this process) but at least the trainees appeared to have a positive learning experience. It is also apparent that they were already thinking about how they could enhance the learning environment for the adult learners they would be training.

Taking Action

Competencies do not change in a vacuum; active engagement in professional, growth-oriented experiences will move the learning process along. It's the only way to go from the X on your career path to the checkmarks along the way to your ultimate career goal.

Create a development plan to increase the probability that you will act. Changing behavior, as discussed earlier in this chapter, requires proceeding through stages of denial, resistance, and exploration to arrive and remain at commitment. It is important to reflect and assess the current stage and take action to move in a productive direction. It may help to begin by selecting activities to improve knowledge and skills in trainer competency areas that have been identified (by yourself and/or others) as needing the greatest development. This will result in the greatest immediate benefit and act as a motivator to continue.

No Classroom, No Facilitator, No Change?

Although delivering training is a much used area of expertise for the training professional, accounting for 17.3 percent of time spent according to the ASTD 2004 Competency Study, it appears to be a competency that is being used less frequently now than in the past. According to the 2006 Industry Report in *Training*, only 62 percent of all training was of the instructor-led classroom variety, low in comparison to the previous year's figures of 70 percent; 15 percent was online self-study, 14 percent was delivered via the virtual classroom, and 9 percent was delivered by other methods. The *2007 State of the Industry Report* (ASTD, 2007) reported 71 percent of training hours available were all instructor-led, as opposed to almost 75 percent in 2004. With such a significant amount of training being conducted via self-study and virtual classroom learning environments, training professionals have less of an opportunity to produce change in employee behavior using traditional classroom training skills. More frequently, they are using technological and organizational forces that support the employee's strong internal motivation to acquire knowledge and skill and change behavior to achieve training goals.

Unfortunately, employees with a bad case of denial and/or resistance are going to be hard-pressed, even in an instructor-led classroom environment, to critically reflect on their preconceived assumptions and beliefs and consciously implement plans to behave differently. The training professional and the organization face a critical challenge to facilitate this segment of the employee population to change their behavior and move into exploring and committing to new ways of performing their jobs. In future chapters, *A Practical Guide to Training and Development* presents strategies and techniques for training professionals to overcome these potentially significant barriers to achieving goals.

CAREER CHALLENGES FOR THE TRAINING PROFESSIONAL

What happens when the training and development person feels the organization is not responsive to change? Trying to facilitate change in a resistant organization can produce a tremendous amount of learning and career development. These professional growth experiences, difficult as they may be at the time, will benefit the training and development person at some point in the future. On the other hand, if the training professional is a member of an organization that embraces and accepts change, it can be a tremendous opportunity to be involved in activities such as participating in training needs assessments, creating training matrices, designing, conducting, and evaluating training programs that become unique learning opportunities. Working in different organizations with both types of cultures—those very resistant to change and those very embracing of change—is probably the most complete learning experience one could ask for. No matter the culture of one's organization, it is in both the training professional's and the organization's best interest to do the best possible job with the situation as it is.

TRAIN EFFECTIVELY OR FACE THE CONSEQUENCES

Organizations cannot afford to miss the mark when providing training. Ineffective or non-existent training programs can lead to serious legal and economic consequences. Training deficiencies can be avoided by effectively implementing strategies to avoid such devastating pitfalls.

Consequences of Ineffective Training

"Truth or Consequences" was the first game show to air on commercially licensed television, appearing on WNBT in 1950. It was an American quiz show originally broadcast on radio beginning in 1940. The entertainment concept was to mix the quiz element of game shows with wacky stunts. Contestants who failed to answer difficult questions correctly, (truth), had to participate in embarrassing stunts (consequences).

Unfortunately, organizations face a similar plight if they do not respond appropriately to training needs. They suffer consequences that are not entertaining; they are embarrassing, costly, and damaging to the ability of the organization to fulfill its mission. Employees who receive inadequate and/or ineffective training can experience similarly dire consequences: disillusionment that may turn into adversarial relationship with employers, physical and psychological disability, even death.

We live in a litigious society. Current statistics of employment lawsuits in the United States illustrate this point. While only a certain percentage of employment lawsuits can be attributed to ineffective training, consider these facts:

- More than 450 employment lawsuits are filed in the United States every day according to a 2006 USA Today report.
- Sixty percent of all companies are sued by former employees every year, according to a 2006 report by the Society for Human Resource Management.
- Eighty percent of all employers sued felt they were the victims of unfair or frivolous lawsuits according to a 2006 survey by the California Chamber of Commerce,
- Half of those companies sued spent in excess of $50,000, and one-third spent more than $100,000 defending against these claims, not including the cost of settlement or verdict, according to the same survey by the Chamber.
- Fifty-six percent of all employment cases that went trial in 2006 resulted in verdicts for the plaintiff (employee).

- $250,000 was the average plaintiff's verdict in employment law cases in 2006, with 15 percent of all verdicts exceeding $1 million.

While it is difficult to assess how many lawsuits could be avoided by effective training, the literature is strewn with unfortunate cases of training efforts (or lack thereof) with negative consequences for both the organization and the trainee. Consider these real, unfortunate cases:

Case 1. In 1999, The Bureau of State Audits presented its report of the California Science Center and concluded that the Center does not ensure fair and equitable treatment of employees, thus exposing the state to risk. Among other deficiencies, the audit found that the organization had an inadequate training program despite regulations that stipulated specific standards. There was no overall training plan or program designed to promote a capable, efficient, and service-oriented workforce. No central training records were kept to document who had received training. It appeared that higher-level employees received more training opportunities than lower level employees, which resulted in some employees being better informed of important policies than others. These factors led to the appearance that the science center treated its employees unfairly and inequitably.

Case 2. In an infamous 1988 case, grocery chain Lucky Stores identified a need for training managers in diversity issues and hired an external trainer to conduct diversity training with the organization's management team. An exercise in the training program asked managers to list various stereotypes they had heard about women and minorities. Their responses were written down on flipchart paper and posted around the room per normal training protocol. Subsequently, female employees of this organization filed a class-action sex discrimination lawsuit against the organization based on a lack of promotions for females. The written comments from the training program were used as evidence in the trial and were found by the court to be not just portrayals of social stereotypes, but reflections of what the managers truly believed. The court concluded that the notes constituted evidence of discriminatory attitudes and stereotyping of women by company managers and awarded the plaintiffs over $90 million in damages.

Case 3. Meyers (2005) reported thirty-one separate incidents across the United States of police officers seriously wounding or killing other police officers in an article titled "Why Are We Killing Ourselves: A Look at Accidental Shootings of Police Officers by Police Officers." At least sixteen of the incidents occurred during training exercises. His analysis concluded that a properly designed and implemented training program would eliminate or minimize the frequency and severity of accidents.

COMMON TRAINING DEFICIENCIES

Unfortunately, poor training outcomes occur for many reasons. Often, their root causes can be grouped into categories that can be readily addressed.

POLICY DOES NOT ENSURE PRACTICE

Organizations make noble gestures. They proclaim in their mission statements, employee handbooks, offer letters, and job descriptions that people are their most treasured resource and that providing training to continually improve knowledge and skills is their highest priority. Walking the talk, however, is another matter. Having a training plan and executing a training plan are two different matters. It is senior management's responsibility to ensure that both planning and execution occur. When they do, training is offered that meets the knowledge and skill improvement needs of employees, and all members of the target audience(s) can participate and benefit from this important activity.

UNREALISTIC EXPECTATIONS

Organizations wrongly assume that training equals behavior change for all participants, that merely sending people to training means that all participants will now perform job tasks the way they have been trained to do. Successful training will accomplish this feat for a great many trainees and for a great many job-related tasks, but assuming 100 percent compliance on both fronts is unrealistic. Less than 100 percent compliance, though, can wreak havoc on an organization. Processes must be put in place to assess individual behavioral change and improved training results once trainees return to their jobs. These same processes will also uncover those individuals for whom training did not produce desired outcomes. A re-training effort for these individuals may be prescribed.

Inadequately Skilled or Unqualified Trainer(s)

After going through the painstaking efforts of training needs identification, securing management support, marketing the training programs to the target audience(s), and internally mobilizing participants to attend, there is nothing more disappointing than a less than effective presenter. Even more distressing and disturbing is an ineffective or unqualified presenter causing an incident in the training program that results in a lawsuit against the organization. The trainer selection process must be given great care and attention regardless of whether the candidate list includes internal employees or external consultants.

Employees are generally known quantities. Carefully assess their knowledge, skill, and readiness to conduct training before they are selected to train others. Just as background checks are conducted on prospective employees, research must be undertaken to make sure the consultant under consideration is qualified to do the job. Check referrals and references from reliable sources, including the consultant's client list, review his or her resume and website, scrutinize training exercises and agenda in advance, and read any of their published books and articles to gather information about the consultant's knowledge and skill. If possible, observe the consultant in action, conducting a training program on the same or similar topic for which the organization is contracting, in front of a live audience.

The trainer must also have extensive knowledge of the relevant organizational policies as well as pertinent local, state, and federal laws and regulations. Providing incorrect or misleading answers to participant questions could lead to misguided behavior and serve as the basis for a future lawsuit. "That's an excellent question. Let me get back to you on that" is a favorite response by trainers if they do not know the answer to a participant's question. It's a much better response than providing wrong information.

Similarly, trainers who are not attorneys should not make statements that suggest a legal opinion. Training participants will sometimes offer so-called hypothetical statements that are actually descriptions of real-life issues occurring in the workplace. For the trainer to respond to such statements by saying, "That's illegal" or "Someone could go to jail for doing that" is inflammatory and could send the wrong message to the participant. Instead, saying something such as "The hypothetical you describe is prohibited by our policy, and anyone who knows someone is behaving in this manner should report it to management" is probably a more appropriate response.

Knowledge and Skill Erosion

Even if 100 percent compliance was achieved and behavioral change was realized at the conclusion of training, time can diminish task performance. People can become complacent, the positive effects of training can wear off, and degraded job performance can result. Re-training on a regular basis can help rekindle peak performance. Frequency of re-training is a judgment call by both management and participants, but should be instituted at mutually agreeable intervals to reinforce behavior. Regularly scheduled, periodic field audits or behavioral observations could be conducted to provide feedback regarding re-training needs.

Failure to Address Important Job Tasks

Certain job tasks within each job classification are more critical than others. Mistakes performing certain responsibilities can be tolerated; for other responsibilities there must be zero tolerance for errors to ensure health and safety. Focus training most acutely on those job tasks for which there can be no deviation from top performance. All too often, training time is not differentiated in this way; concentrate efforts on critical tasks to ensure behavioral compliance.

Transmissional Not Transformational Learning

Training that only imparts information and knowledge does not necessarily translate into behavioral change. Frequently, instructor-led classroom training as well as self-paced learning is designed to stream information to participants without paying particular attention to interaction and new behavioral practice. Self-paced training delivered via computer or teleconference is much less likely to afford opportunities to practice behavior change. Organizations need to ensure, as best they can, that training is enhancing knowledge and skills and achieving the goal of changing behavior. Build opportunities to demonstrate and practice desired new behaviors into the training design (incorporating the adult learning Law of Exercise, as seen in Chapter 5) to help the transformational process.

Incomplete or Non-Existent Evaluation

An evaluation process at the behavioral and results level (see Chapter 7) reveals whether knowledge and skill enhancement have translated into behavioral change and improved results. If behavioral- and results-level evaluation is not instituted, there is no data to support the contention that task performance has been raised as a result of training. Attending training does not necessarily equal heightened performance by participants.

Positive evaluative feedback from trainee reactions is a start. Self-reported improvement in learning is good. Testing to validate learning achievements is better. Participants stating unequivocally that they will behave differently if or when faced with certain critical incidents in the future is important to know. But none of these evaluation criteria will truly reveal whether on-the-job behavior has changed. Only evaluation processes conducted at the behavioral and/or results level will reveal that change has occurred.

Inconsistent Management Support

Management support is vital for successful training. Managers can ensure that all of their direct reports attend training as scheduled. They can also encourage trainees to demonstrate newly learned behavior on the job once they return to the front line. Managers can also notice and praise new and improved behavior. All too often, though, management support is inconsistent. Some managers ensure 100 percent attendance; others overtly and/or covertly make it difficult for their direct reports to participate. Some managers support the attendees' desire to try new behavior; other managers barely acknowledge the attendees' participation in training and ignore or even discourage any new behavior based on newly learned knowledge and skill. Supportive management behavior must be consistent in all regards. Senior management must instill this value with all of their direct reports. Managers attending their own program that focuses on methods of supporting organizational training makes a statement that new trainee behavior is expected and encouraged after attending training.

Lack of Individual Responsibility

Organizations must fulfill their responsibility to provide high-quality training and to support 100 percent participation by the target audience(s). But, as the expression goes, "You can lead a horse to water but you can't make him drink." Employees must share equally in the responsibility by continuing to acquire knowledge and skill to maintain job behavior and performance at maximum effectiveness. There is no place for denial and/or resistance to training when diminished job performance puts people's lives, including the trainees,' at risk. Complacency or assuming an attitude of knowing it all can only lead to trouble for the employee and the organization.

Effective Training for Minimized Liability

Just as ineffective or non-existent training can lead to dire consequences, effective training is an ally to everyone—non-supervisory employees, managers, executives, investors, and customers. It produces productive changes in knowledge, skills, attitude and behavior that contribute to accomplishing strategic goals. Additionally, these changes will lead to better behavioral choices by trainees that by their nature minimize legal risk. However, if an employee's actions are challenged in court, the fact that the organization had a training program in place may minimize liability if certain requirements are met.

Exercising Reasonable Care

The courts generally look more kindly on employers who can demonstrate that they took actions to minimize the potential for negative outcomes. One way to demonstrate this good faith effort is through training. When an employer can show that the accused employee(s) participated in a training program (via dated sign-in sheets) that covered relevant information (via training agenda and program materials) taught by a knowledgeable trainer (via his or her professional work experience resume) but behaved badly nevertheless, it strengthens the employer's case that it truly attempted to instill positive behavior. This circumstance also underscores the importance of strong management support for training, thus ensuring that all members of the target audience attend training. If someone did not attend the training and is alleged to have behaved badly, the organization's liability is not mitigated.

Adequate Training

To minimize liability, training must also be perceived as adequate. Employees accused of wrongdoing who describe their training experience with the organization in vague, sketchy, and nondescriptive terms would not give the impression that the training they received was adequate. While training is difficult to plan and challenging to execute, the organization must ensure that adequate time and resources are devoted to creating a training curriculum that participants will learn from and use in their daily job tasks.

Management of Training Room Behavior: An Example

Inappropriate comments made by attendees that suggest stereotypes, bias, and/or hostility toward others have been used as evidence of hostile work environments in claims of discrimination by employees who are the targets of such epithets. These are serious issues that must be addressed in order to minimize risk and send the proper message to participants. The following suggested strategies will minimize (or eliminate) the opportunity for such inappropriate behavior during training;

1. At the beginning of each session, the trainer lists behavioral ground rules, including guidelines prohibiting discriminatory speech.
2. If such words are spoken during the training, trainers must immediately intervene, stating that the comment is not appropriate for the workplace and does not represent the viewpoint of the organization. Saying something like "While we may have our own personal opinions on these sorts of issues, what was said is a perfect example of something not to say" sends the proper message to the other trainees and should prevent future similar future expressions.
3. If certain people do not heed the warning and continue to make inappropriate statements, the trainer must remove the individual(s) from the room.

CLEAR LINES OF ORGANIZATIONAL ACCOUNTABILITY AND RESPONSIBILITY

One person must be in charge of training if a court of law is to view the function favorably. The enterprise's organizational chart should clearly delineate a person who has training responsibility. This is the individual responsible for making budgetary decisions related to training expenditures and accountable for the development and execution of a training plan.

Courts will tend to view the training function skeptically and as an uncontrolled activity if no one in the organization is ultimately held accountable for its actions. Liability is minimized through effective training, and the opportunity to create an effective training function is greatly enhanced with a clearly defined, accountable, and responsible training leader.

ACCESSIBLE TO ALL

For training to be effective, it is important to make sure that all trainees can understand the content of the program. It is difficult to expect knowledge and skill improvement from all trainees if language, hearing, or visual impairments interfere with communication. Provide reasonable accommodations to ensure that all receive the training messages accurately. Examples of such accommodations can include training conducted in languages other than English, using sign language interpreters, and/or providing written materials in large print or Braille. Ensure that the training location is wheelchair accessible. These aids will ensure access and the ability to communicate with all trainees. The training professional could conduct an assessment to identify the necessary accommodations to include all trainees.

EVALUATION FOLLOW-UP

As described later in the book, using learning, behavioral, and results criteria is vital to provide evaluative data documenting the impact of the training program on the individuals attending. Of course, the trainer hopes that all attendees will show post-training improvements.

Organizations that collect this sort of training data and then do not counsel or re-train participants who don't improve could be liable for charges of negative retention if these same individuals behave badly afterward. For training to limit, not create, liability, the organization must act on this information once it is available to ensure that it is doing all it can to improve the knowledge and skill of all employees.

Summary

1. Training helps employees do their current jobs more effectively; development helps prepare employees for their next opportunity.

2. The two essential training elements are facilitating change and achieving goals.

3. Employees progress through four stages of change; denial, resistance, exploration and commitment.

4. The role of the trainer involves mastery of foundational competencies, developing areas of professional expertise and assuming various organizational roles.

5. Competencies are developed by undertaking a variety of professional development activities.

6. Organizations experience severe consequences by conducting ineffective training.

7. Organizations must overcome training deficiencies and provide effective training to minimize liability.

CHAPTER TWO

ALIGNING TRAINING WITH VISION, MISSION, AND GOALS

"When you're finished changing, you're finished."
BENJAMIN FRANKLIN

PURPOSE

This chapter will enable you to accomplish the following:

- Distinguish *"vision"* from *"mission"*
- Examine the value of establishing and aligning vision, mission, and goals
- Discuss the contributions of two experts (Deming and Drucker) to the search for keys to organizational success
- Recognize training's role in supporting the organization's strategies for success
- Discuss the importance of organizational goals

OVERVIEW

Organizations create strategies and structures to meet and exceed their performance expectations. While there is not a singular formula for achieving this goal, organizations have adopted and modified the principles, research, and recommendations of experts in business and management to formulate their own plans for achieving and maintaining success. Training and development play a pivotal role in facilitating the successful implementation of the organization's strategic plans.

This chapter presents the widely accepted and utilized practice of creating vision statements, mission statements, and strategic goals to focus employee behavior in the quest to achieve performance expectations. The chapter will discuss aligning training with goals as well as the important role that goals play in shaping behavior.

Finding a Formula for Success

It is the goal of every organization to be successful. Organizations define success in different ways. Generally speaking, organizations consider themselves successful if they meet or exceed their own performance expectations.

Organizations continuously search for and adopt methods to improve performance and remain successful. Customarily, it is senior management's responsibility to create and promulgate strategies, a set of internal structures, and standards that serve to guide everyone's actions on a long- and short-term basis. An organization's success often hinges on its strategies and ability to focus the behavior of all organization members to support its strategies and the goals it is hoping to achieve.

There is no one set of business strategies that guarantees success. In the 1940s and 1950s, renowned experts such as W. Edwards Deming and Peter Drucker conducted extensive studies of organizations and formulated their recommendations for success that were published in their books and articles. In the 1960s, the emergence of successful Japanese companies, heavily influenced by the theories of Deming and Drucker, led to subsequent adoption of their practices by more American companies than had previously subscribed to these theories. Deming's 14 Points and Drucker's Management by Objectives have been refined and modified over the years by such authors as Jim Collins and Donald Wheeler, but the original practitioners are still well-respected and their theories still serve as cornerstones of business strategies throughout the world today. Many organizations still adhere to the principles promulgated by Deming and Drucker.

W. EDWARDS DEMING

W. Edwards Deming was born in Sioux City, Iowa, and earned a B.S. in electrical engineering from the University of Wyoming, an M.S. from the University of Colorado and a Ph.D. from Yale University, after which he interned at Bell Laboratories. Both graduate degrees were in mathematics and physics. Deming went to Japan after World War II to help set up a census of the Japanese population. While he was there, he taught statistical process control (SPC) methods to Japanese business leaders and engineers. SPC, pioneered by Walter Shewhart in the early 1920s and applied by Deming in the United States during World War II, is an effective method of monitoring a process by collecting data at various points within the process and analyzing variations in output. The end result is manufacturing high-quality goods while reducing waste, increasing the likelihood of customer satisfaction because problems will not be passed along to the customer (or end-user) of the product and/or service.

Deming witnessed Japan's extraordinary economic growth, watching them put into practice the methods he had taught. He stressed that improved quality would result in reduced expenses, increased productivity and market share. In 1960 he was awarded a medal by the Japanese Emperor and is regarded by many observers as having more impact on Japanese business than any individual not of Japanese descent. He later became a professor at New York University and a consultant in Washington, D.C., to government and business leaders.

From 1979 to 1982 the Ford Motor Company incurred more than $3 billion in debt. Deming went to work for the company in 1981. After adopting Deming's principles as well as focusing on changing management behavior and organizational culture, Ford became the most profitable American auto company, exceeding the earnings of arch rival General Motors for the first time since the 1920s.

In the midst of his work with Ford, Deming published *Quality, Productivity, and Competitive Position* (1982), which was renamed *Out of the Crisis* (1986) and included his now famous 14 Points for Management. He believed that these philosophies, if adopted by the manufacturing sector, would save the United States from industrial doom at the hands of the Japanese. Paraphrasing Deming's 14 points, he stated the following:

1. "Create constancy of purpose toward improvement." Replace short-term reaction with long-term planning to be competitive and stay in business. Decide to whom top management is responsible.
2. "Adopt the new philosophy." No longer accept current level of delays, mistakes, defective materials, and defective workmanship. The implication is that management should actually adopt this philosophy, and a philosophy of cooperation between employees, management, customers, and suppliers, rather than merely expecting the workforce to adopt a new philosophy.
3. "Cease dependence on inspection." Instead, require statistical evidence that quality is built in. If variation is reduced, the need to inspect manufactured items for defects is unnecessary because there won't be any. Prevent defects instead of trying to detect them.
4. "Move toward a single supplier for any one item." Multiple suppliers means greater opportunity for variation in source product quality. Depend on meaningful measures of quality along with price. Eliminate suppliers that cannot qualify with statistical evidence of quality.
5. "Improve constantly and forever." Constantly strive to reduce variation. Find problems
6. "Institute training on the job." If people are inadequately trained, they will not all work the same way, and this will introduce variation.
7. "Institute leadership." There is a difference between leadership and supervision, the latter being quota and target based. Shift to a focus on quality which will automatically improve productivity. Management must take immediate action when alerted to process problems.
8. "Drive out fear." Management by fear is counter-productive in the long term because it prevents employees from acting in the organization's best interests.
9. "Break down barriers between departments." Producing a quality product and/or service for the external customer is

a team effort that requires cooperation inside the organization. The concept of the internal customer is reinforced when each department serves other departments that use its outputs.

10. "Eliminate slogans." It's not people who make the most mistakes—it's the process they are working within. Harassing the workforce with exhortations without improving the processes they use is counter-productive.

11. "Eliminate management by objectives." Production targets encourage the delivery of a quota of quality products and services without regard to their quality.

12. "Remove barriers to pride of workmanship." Pride of workmanship increases employee satisfaction.

13. "Institute a vigorous program of education and self-improvement for everyone."

14. "The transformation is everyone's job." Create a top management structure that will push everyday on the previous thirteen points.

Deming received criticism for his 14 Points for Management because he did not include implementation tools to help bring his management philosophy to fruition. When asked why he didn't provide this sort of assistance, his response was "You're the manager; you figure it out."

Donald Wheeler, Ph.D., is the author of more than fifteen books and more than sixty articles in the field of statistical process control. He had the good fortune to work with Deming from 1981 to 1993 and is credited with continuing to refine Deming's work, applying his theories and concepts to current business practices as a consulting statistician. In Wheeler's book *Understanding Statistical Process Control* (1992), Deming writes the foreword and says, "It is fitting to add my deep appreciation for the mathematical achievement of Dr. Wheeler. His understanding of theory, and its application, is guided by mathematical knowledge."

Peter Drucker

Peter Drucker was born in Vienna, Austria, and earned a doctorate in international law from Frankfurt University in 1931. The rise of Nazism forced him to leave Germany in 1933, and in 1937 he moved permanently to the United States, where he became a university professor and freelance writer about business practices. His writings won him access to the internal workings of General Motors (GM), one of the biggest organizations in the world at that time. The resulting book, *Concept of the Corporation,* popularized the multidivisional organizational structure used by GM with all its systems and management challenges. This book led to numerous professional articles, consulting engagements, and research projects. Drucker authored thirty-nine books in his lifetime. He taught at New York University as a professor of management from 1950 to 1971. From 1971 until his death in 2005, he was the Clarke Professor of Social Science and Management at Claremont Graduate University. From 1975 to 1995 he was an editorial columnist for *The Wall Street Journal* and was a frequent contributor to the *Harvard Business Review.*

Drucker was most interested in employees who knew more about certain aspects of the organization than their bosses and yet needed to cooperate with others in a large enterprise to perform their jobs effectively. In *Landmarks of Tomorrow: A Report on the New 'Post Modern' World* (1959), he coined the term *knowledge worker,* one who works primarily with information or one who develops and uses knowledge in the workplace. He is credited with unknowingly ushering in what we now call *the knowledge economy,* focused on the production and management of knowledge. It is the title of Chapter 12 of his book *The Age of Discontinuity* (1969). Drucker believed that if organizations were unsuccessful, it was because they used outdated ideas, had a narrow conception of their problems, or experienced internal misunderstandings.

He wrote extensively about *management by objectives,* stating in *The Practice of Management* (1954) that "business performance requires that each job be directed toward the objectives of the whole business." Further, he wrote in the same book that "objectives are needed in every area where performance and results directly and vitally affect the survival and prosperity of the business."

Jim Collins, best-selling author of *Good to Great* and co-author of *Built to Last,* wrote a November 28, 2005, article in *Business-Week.* In which he stated that he went to Claremont, California, in 1994 seeking wisdom from the greatest management thinker of our age. He came away feeling that he'd met a compassionate and generous human being who was driven not by the desire to say something but by the desire to learn something from every student he met. And that, Collins said, is why "he became one of the most influential teachers most of us have ever known."

VISION, MISSION, AND GOAL ALIGNMENT

Many organizations subscribe to a business strategy that emanates from a plan that aligns and supports the vision, the mission, enterprise-wide strategic goals, department goals, and individual goals. Conceptually, such a strategy works in a cascading fashion (Figure 2.1):

FIGURE 2.1. ALIGNING VISION, MISSION, AND GOALS

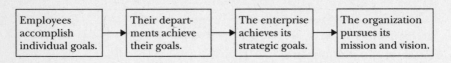

VISION AND MISSION

A *vision statement,* a one-sentence pronouncement of a desired future state, articulates what the organization hopes to become. It can be as simple as "to be an award-winning, best-in-class dance studio." A mission statement flows from the vision statement and clarifies what an organization does via its product and/or service. "Providing ongoing high-quality dance instruction" could be the dance studio's mission statement. Both vision and mission statements are intentionally strong on focus and intent but weak on specifics.

ENTERPRISE-WIDE STRATEGIC GOALS

Specifics come in the form of enterprise-wide strategic goals that identify key performance areas. When measured against actual organizational performance, they help determine whether an organization is meeting or even exceeding its own expectations. For instance, the dance studio may have strategic goals that

1. Identify ten specific awards it plans to win in nationwide competitions that year
2. Target a 90 percent customer satisfaction level as measured by its customer opinion surveys
3. Project top-quartile marks for quality dance instruction as measured by an audit conducted by a local college dance program
4. Increase the number of students by 5 percent each year

If the studio is meeting or exceeding performance in each of these four strategic goals, it is successfully pursuing its vision and mission.

DEPARTMENT GOALS

Enterprise-wide strategic goals are more likely to be achieved when departmental goal accomplishment supports strategic goals accomplishment. The critical performance measures are what each department strives to meet to support enterprise-wide strategic goals. Naturally, department goals depend on the function of the department.

The goals of the dance studio's instructor department (i.e., levels of dancer/customer satisfaction, entry/placement in X number of nationwide dance competitions) are different from those of the customer service and collections department. Customer service and collections department goals (i.e., levels of external customer satisfaction, outstanding accounts receivable) are different from the goals of the sales and marketing department (i.e., number of newly signed up dance students, number and quality of marketing pieces in the newspaper). The goals of the human resources department (i.e., levels of internal customer/employee satisfaction, quality of newly hired dance instructors) are different from the goals of the finance department (i.e., profit margins, year-over-year profit/loss ratios). In fact, there is often a dynamic tension between the goals of the individual departments, meaning that one department's goals are sometimes in opposition to another department's goals. For instance, when the sales and marketing department wants to acquire more dance students by cutting fees, increasing advertising, and providing promotions and incentives, that tactic may work against the goal of the finance department to maintain profit margins. These conflicts make for interesting senior manager meetings!

When departments meet and/or exceed their goals, they contribute to the organization meeting its enterprise-wide strategic goals.

INDIVIDUAL GOALS

Departmental goals are more likely to be achieved when individuals accomplish goals that support accomplishing departmental goals. The critical metrics that each employee strives to meet should support departmental goals (which in turn support enterprise-wide strategic goals, mission and vision). Naturally, individual goals depend on the employee's role in the organization.

Dance instructor goals might include achieving high levels of dancer (customer) satisfaction, providing high-quality instruction that showcases student talents, and frequent high placement in dance competitions. Customer service representative goals might include consistently demonstrating phone behavior that results in high levels of customer satisfaction, handling a requisite volume of phone calls, and successfully collecting monies owed to the dance studio. Sales and marketing representative goals might include signing up a certain number of dance students each month and generating a certain number of newspaper articles about the dance studio per quarter. Human resource representative goals might include achieving a certain percentage of highly satisfied internal customers/employees and interviewing a certain number of candidates per month to fill open positions. The finance analyst's goals might include producing monthly reports that track key statistics in order to help make decisions regarding incentives and expenditures.

When employees meet and/or exceed their individual goals, they contribute to their department's achieving its goals.

Training's Supportive Role

Training and development support the organization's vision, mission, and enterprise-wide strategic goal achievement by facilitating positive changes in employee knowledge, skills, attitudes, and behaviors that improve job performance and thus contribute to overall organizational performance. One of Deming's 14 Points for transforming business effectiveness, discussed earlier in this chapter, was to "institute training for skills." Further, he went on to say "there is no substitute for knowledge."

Well-trained dance instructors, those with improved knowledge, skills, attitudes, and behaviors, will perform their jobs more effectively than less-well-trained dance instructors will. A dance studio with well-trained instructors stands a much better chance than a studio of less-well-trained instructors of winning the requisite number of awards, achieving high customer satisfaction levels, and passing the college audit with flying colors. Along with well-trained customer service representatives, sales and marketing representatives, human resource representatives, and financial analysts, this dance studio organization has a great opportunity to achieve ongoing success.

Consider the examples below of vision and mission statements and enterprise-wide strategic goals (company name and specific performance metrics omitted). Opportunity abounds for training to focus on the employee's job-related knowledge, skills, attitudes, and behaviors that will improve individual job performance and the organization's potential success. Training topics offered to employees would depend on the results of the needs assessment (see next chapter), but the vision, mission, and strategic goal statements suggest potential areas of training focus.

Example 1

The vision of our organization is to be the leading supplier of advanced turnkey (instantly usable) solutions to retailers so they can become more profitable. Our mission is to provide high-quality functional application programs on a timely basis to the industry by . . . (1) creating a passionate, profit oriented selling environment as measured by (2) developing a highly competent, customer-oriented professional workforce as measured by. . . .

Example 2

Our vision is to be the leading pharmaceutical and drug delivery company with a focus in the high-growth U.S. market. Our mission is to provide safe, effective drugs and therapies that improve the quality of life for our customers worldwide. The company is pursuing these initiatives through two major strategies:(1) licensing, acquiring and developing late-stage pharmaceuticals for marketing to high-prescribing physicians as measured by . . . (2) developing a proprietary drug delivery system as measured by. . . .

Example 3

Our vision is to be a successful international baked goods company. Our mission is to produce great tasting, healthy products. We strive to fulfill our vision and mission by (1) having integrity in everything we do as measured by . . .(2) providing excellent customer service as measured by . . . (3) using quality ingredients as measured by . . . (4) offering a clean and friendly environment as measured by . . . (5) demonstrating commitment to our employees and business associates as measured by. . . .

Example 4

The vision of our practice is to be the preferred provider of audiology-related services to physicians and patients in our geographic location. Our mission is helping individuals hear better by providing ongoing professional and caring audiological services. Our strategic goals are to (1) exceed patient and physician expectations on X percent of our customer satisfaction surveys; (2) reduce our product return rate by a minimum of X percent over the previous year; (3) increase our net revenue by a minimum of X percent over the previous year.

Each vision and mission statement and enterprise-wide strategic goal represents opportunities for training to focus on facilitating positive changes to employee knowledge, skill, attitude, and behavior and contribute to the organization's strategic goal achievement. The question arises as to the knowledge bases, skill sets, attitudes, and behaviors that training should focus on.

DETERMINING TRAINING PRIORITIES

Employees possess wide ranges of knowledge and skills and demonstrate diverse attitudes and behaviors during a typical work day. Because the training function has limits like any other organizational resource, it is essential for training to set priorities and focus on select knowledge, skills, attitude, and behavioral areas that will produce the most benefit to the organization for the training intervention.

A comprehensive training needs assessment process, discussed in the next chapter, will help determine the priority of changes in knowledge, skill, attitude, and behavior that will provide the greatest impact on achieving goals. The needs assessment results will help determine training's priority topic(s), target audience(s), goals, and course content.

THE IMPORTANCE OF ORGANIZATIONAL GOALS

Goals can influence behavior. Whether setting a personal goal ("I need to lose ten pounds by summer") or a professional goal ("I need to train all employees in sexual harassment prevention by year-end'), goals can serve as calls-to-action to achieve desired results.

A key qualifier is the word "can." Behavior drives performance, but does not automatically follow goal setting (if weight loss were only that easy!). Organizational behavior can be influenced, even driven, by goals. Goals are invaluable tools for organizational success when used properly; then they can become (in Lewin's terms) driving forces that support and maintain newly changed behavior. Applied improperly, goals can become restraining forces that undo changed behavior and bring back a state of equilibrium.

EFFECTIVE GOAL FORMULATION AND APPLICATION

Goals must contain certain attributes in order to be implemented successfully. These important factors help make goals integral to successful organization performance.

Written

Goals should be communicated in writing so they can be displayed in a prominent place as a constant reminder. Verbally communicated goals aren't displayable, and they tend to be forgotten or remembered differently than originally intended.

If the goal of training all employees in sexual harassment prevention by year-end is written and taped to the wall of the trainer's office or cubicle, it is a clear, daily reminder of a goal that must be achieved by a specific date.

SMART Goals

Smart goals are clear and concise and therefore more likely to be understood. The components of SMART goals are

- **Specific.** Targeting a single result as in "train all employees in sexual harassment prevention" makes the goal easy to understand.
- **Measurable.** Including a measurement to determine whether the goal has been reached ensures that goal achievement can be evaluated. Reviewing sexual harassment prevention training sign-in sheets will determine whether all employees have attended if that is a stated goal.
- **Attainable.** Goals that employees can achieve motivate behavior. Goals that are unrealistic frustrate employees and serve no purpose. Organization size, logistics, and culture are a few of the factors that will determine whether all employees can be trained in sexual harassment prevention by year-end.
- **Role-Related.** Goals that are role-related can be influenced, even controlled, by the employee attempting to achieve such a goal. The trainer can schedule enough sexual harassment training sessions to ensure that everyone is scheduled to attend by year-end. Getting them there is another story. The trainer may need to use the interpersonal competency role of "influencing stakeholders" with the management team to ensure that all employees attend when scheduled.
- **Time-Bound.** Deadlines create a sense of urgency and closure. Without a due date, the goal does not exist. Year-end usually means by December 31 of the current calendar year. In this

case, training all employees in sexual harassment prevention by year-end means by December 31.

There was once an employee who was assigned a project in July with a goal to accomplish it by year-end. In December, when it was clear the project would not be completed on time, he was confronted by his manager and asked why he did not finish the project by year-end. He told his manager he thought the deadline was year-end of the following year. The employee understood the concept of year-end very clearly when his employment was terminated on December 31.

Tied to Performance Management Systems. Goals drive behavior when there is a reward for achieving them. The reward can be extrinsic, such as a monetary or tangible bonus or perquisite. Or the reward can be intrinsic in that it just feels good to achieve the goal. Regardless, the person striving to complete the goal needs to buy in to it and understand WIIFM to be motivated. Goals are a cornerstone of performance management systems; they are integral to establishing standards of work performance/ performance expectations, measuring and monitoring ongoing work performance, summarizing end-of-year performance by conducting performance evaluations, and determining future performance levels.

Goals are also vital when addressing work performance that is not meeting performance expectations. Goals serve as an objective standard that the employee must strive to meet in order to remain a viable and productive member of the organization's team. Formal counseling and appropriate corrective action are discussed and documented in terms of the performance goals that have been established for the behavior in question. They become the basis for a legal defense if the employer's actions are challenged in court.

The trainer knows that the goal of training all employees in sexual harassment prevention by year-end is one of several goals that will be reviewed as part of the annual performance evaluation process. Completing all goals will mean a significant merit pay increase. Therefore, the trainer is strongly motivated to accomplish all goals on time.

Employee Involvement. Involving employees in the formulation of goals assists with their buy-in and increases their motivation to behave accordingly. Top-down goals that don't involve employees are less likely to serve their purpose. Management has the responsibility to set goals and should not agree to a goal that doesn't serve the best interests of the whole organization. But discussion and compromise with employees who must meet the goals usually leads to a better outcome for all involved.

The training manager discussed the goal of training all employees in sexual harassment prevention with the trainer during the goal setting portion of the performance evaluation process. The trainer felt very comfortable agreeing to this goal.

Periodic Progress Checks. Periodically monitoring goal accomplishment status helps determine whether performance is proceeding according to plan. Progress can be acknowledged and problems can be addressed as necessary. Also, if business conditions and organizational priorities change, performance goals can be altered and/or renegotiated to address new circumstances.

On a monthly basis, the training manager reviewed with the trainer progress toward the goal of training all employees in sexual harassment prevention by year-end. The trainer indicated that some departments were very cooperative and compliant in making sure their employees attended training when scheduled. The trainer also indicated that some departments were not cooperating in sending their people to the training. The training manager said he would speak with his managerial peers to resolve the issue. The trainer said he would schedule a limited number of additional training sessions to accommodate those who had missed the training the first time around. Both agreed that business conditions dictated that the goal would remain in effect.

Consistency Among Employees. Employees with same or similar job titles and responsibilities should have attainable goals that reflect their years of job-related work experience. More experienced employees should have higher goals that those for new employees.

The goal of training all employees in sexual harassment prevention by year-end was achievable for the more experienced trainer. The goal of conducting new employee orientation on an as-needed basis was achievable for the less experienced trainer.

Goal Alignment. Goals should be aligned so that employees achieving their individual goals will contribute to their department's achieving its goals. Department goal achievement should contribute to the achievement of enterprise-wide strategic goals. Enterprise-wide strategic goals achievement should support the organization's mission and vision. Each member of the enterprise contributes something different, but everyone's efforts must pull in the same direction toward a common goal if the organization is to be successful.

The trainer goal of training all employees in sexual harassment prevention by year-end contributes to the training department's goal of providing training programs on priority topics as determined by the organization's annual training needs assessment. Fulfilling the training department's goal contributes to the enterprise-wide strategic goal of high employee satisfaction by actively supporting a harassment-free work environment. The enterprise-wide strategic goal supports the organization's mission and vision that articulates the crucial contribution that employees make to the organization's success.

Tools for Overcoming Denial and Resistance. Goals are tools that can effectively support behavior change to overcome denial and resistance. Behavioral goals can provide an expectation of job performance that the employee, stuck in denial and/or resistance, can view as an attainable next step. Short-term goals break down what might seem to be an insurmountable end result with intermediate steps that are achievable.

If the trainer had been in denial/resistance, the goal of training all employees in sexual harassment prevention by year-end would have been viewed as insurmountable. Establishing a short-term goal of conducting one sexual harassment prevention training program per week with an average of twenty-five employees attending each session would have been viewed as attainable. It would have had the desired effect of moving the trainer out of denial/resistance and into exploration and ultimately commitment to the goal of training all employees in sexual harassment prevention by year-end.

Barriers to Achieving Goals

Organizations generally take great care and spend enormous amounts of time and thought defining, communicating, measuring, monitoring, maintaining, and improving a business strategy that often includes a vision statement, mission statement, and goals. The system is intended to focus all employee efforts on the common purpose of making the enterprise successful. If goals are not clearly defined, effectively communicated and/or continually measured and monitored, the process of overcoming barriers will be inhibited.

Deficiencies in knowledge and skill as well as unproductive attitudes and behaviors will hinder goal achievement at the strategic, departmental, and/or individual level. The training and development work must focus on supporting positive change in employee knowledge, skills, attitudes, and behavior to remove barriers to accomplishing the organization's goals.

A comprehensive training needs assessment process identifies areas in which change is necessary. The training professional will use interpersonal, business/management, and personal competencies to undertake this crucial project. Chapter 3 discusses the needs assessment process that helps clarify and prioritize training needs and the performance changes that need to occur.

Summary

1. Organizations consider themselves successful if they meet or exceed their own performance expectations.

2. Organizations still apply the business and management theories of W. Edwards Deming and Peter Drucker.

3. Vision, mission, and strategic goal alignment is a common business strategy used by many organizations to strive for maximum performance.

4. Training supports the organization's vision, mission, and enterprise-wide strategic goal achievement by facilitating positive changes in employee knowledge, skills, attitudes, and behaviors that improve job performance and thus contribute to overall organizational performance.

5. A training needs assessment process helps determine the priority of changes in knowledge, skill, attitude and behavior that will provide the greatest impact on achieving goals.

6. Goals are invaluable tools for organizational success because, when used properly, they drive and support new behavior.

CHAPTER THREE

NEEDS ASSESSMENT

"If we don't change direction soon, we'll end up where we're going."
PROFESSOR IRWIN COREY, COMEDIAN

PURPOSE

This chapter will enable you to accomplish the following:

* Recognize the important role that needs assessment plays in focusing training resources
* Differentiate between macro and micro model processes to determine training needs
* Examine a case study that reviews training needs assessment result trends
* Identify processes that organize and rank training needs data

OVERVIEW

An organized approach is necessary to identify and fulfill training needs. Organizations spend billions of dollars annually on training—$129.6 billion in 2006, according to ASTD's *2007 State of the Industry Report*. With such a sizable investment, organizations must use a process to prioritize and focus training resources.

Organizations can use many methods and tools to identify training needs. This chapter describes two different processes, in a linear, step-by-step manner that both arrive at the same destination—identified training needs. Training needs assessments uncover the many changes needed for an organization to achieve its goals. Some changes are achievable using a training intervention, others are not. Some changes are more critical than others. This chapter will demonstrate a useful tool called a selection grid, a method to categorize and prioritize issues and focus on the most critical changes first.

Training Wants Versus Training Needs

The song lyric says, "You can't always get what you want, but if you try sometime, you might find, you can get what you need." With apologies to the Rolling Stones' Mick Jagger and Keith Richards, an organization can get all the training it wants on just about any topic imaginable. *Training's* 2005 Industry Report and its exclusive analysis of employer-sponsored training in the United States listed twenty-nine different training topics offered by organizations. An unpublished research study by Moskowitz (2007) of 314 training needs assessments conducted from 1991 to 2006 uncovered forty-nine distinct training topics that organizations identified on their training wish list. Organizations must determine their training priorities to achieve the maximum return on this sizable resource investment.

Using Macro and Micro Models to Identify Training Needs

Organizations can use many different processes and tools to identify training needs and determine the training they require. Training priorities can be based on a macro model that views the organization's entire business strategy and attempts to strengthen areas supporting strategic goal accomplishment as well as make changes to employee knowledge, skills, attitudes, and behavior to mitigate performance barriers. Or training priorities can also be determined by applying a micro model that uses a task analysis approach and focuses facilitating changes to employee knowledge, skills, attitudes and behavior based on rating performance ability and task necessity levels in "key result areas" (KRAs). KRAs are the crucial aspects of a job for which performance indicators are created, monitored, and used to determine an employee's overall job performance.

Aspects of both macro and micro models may be combined to determine training needs. Each approach has the potential for success; each has strengths and weaknesses. As the song (sort of) goes, you can always get the training you want, but if you try sometime, you might find, you can get the training you need.

STRATEGIC GOAL METHOD: A MACRO MODEL

The macro-model approach to identifying training needs focuses on the organization's overall vision, mission, and enterprise-wide strategic goals. The purpose of the strategic goal process is to find out, from as many people in the organization as possible, the strengths they believe support organization performance as well as the barriers they think prevent the organization from achieving maximum performance. Using a combination of one-on-one interviews, surveys and tapping into other sources of organizational information, this assessment model will uncover the knowledge, skill, attitude, and behavior changes that need to occur for the organization to achieve its goals and fulfill both its vision and mission.

Gathering Information from Management. The training professional must first meet with the CEO, probably the person most focused and passionate about the organization's vision and mission. If there is time for only two questions, they should be

1. What knowledge, skills, attitudes and behaviors help support our vision and mission and
2. What knowledge, skills, attitudes, and behaviors are barriers to our vision and mission?

Because accuracy is all-important, write down all of the CEO's responses immediately. Waiting to make notes until after the meeting risks recall error.

The training professional must meet one-on-one with each member of the senior management team as well since these are the people who are probably most responsible and interested in the organization achieving one or more of its enterprise-wide strategic goals. Again, if time permits only two questions, they should be

1. What knowledge, skills, attitudes, and behaviors support our strategic goal achievement and
2. What knowledge, skills, attitudes, and behaviors are barriers to our strategic goal achievement?

Again, write down all verbal responses during each meeting.

Depending on the size and demographics of the organization, the training professional should try to organize a one-on-one meeting with each department manager since these are the people in the organization most focused on their departments achieving their goals. Again, if time permits only two questions, they should be

1. What knowledge, skills, attitudes and behaviors support department goal achievement and
2. What knowledge, skills, attitudes, and behaviors are barriers to department goal achievement?

Again, write down all responses immediately.

If the training professional begins the information-gathering process with the CEO, or the highest-ranking accessible member of the organization, the rest of the management team will get the message that this is an important meeting they need to make time for. Training professionals have learned from experience that the management team is likely to expound and discuss many more topics than strictly answering these two questions. This is good.

It is an opportunity for each member of the senior management team to articulate their perceptions of the organization's overall strengths and challenges and the integral role that training can play to provide strategic support and value. These conversations have the effect of exploring and confirming the important roles and potential benefits that training can provide. Training becomes more than an obligation and a mandatory expense in the eyes of a skeptical management team member. It becomes a business partner that is a resource to be used to help accomplish business goals.

GATHERING INFORMATION FROM MANAGEMENT: A CASE STUDY

The manager of staff education and development at the University of California San Diego was fortunate to have this conversation every year with Chancellor Richard Atkinson, the CEO of the campus in the 1980s. In an extensive one-on-one conversation, he would ask Dr. Atkinson what was getting in the way of UCSD achieving its purpose. Dr. Atkinson's insights were extremely important because a key role of the manager of staff education and development was to design, conduct, and evaluate training programs for staff.

Wonderfully, Dr. Atkinson would expound on his points, turning the planned fifteen-minute meeting into a forty-five-minute discussion. He was the stereotypically brilliant absent-minded professor; his mind was everywhere.

Anyone meeting with him was always warned not to be insulted if he suddenly left the meeting to make or take a phone call because, if something occurred to him, he had to deal with it right away. But Dr. Atkinson never left his meeting with the manager of staff education and development. He was interested and engaged in the subject matter. And the vice chancellors were very warm and welcoming to the manager of staff education and development when he met with each of them.

CEO and Senior Management Receptivity. CEOs and senior managers in many organizations would welcome the opportunity to have this sort of conversation with the training professional if it resulted in a more organized and more focused training effort, higher organizational performance, and a greater return on a considerable training investment. Having this conversation with one of the highest-ranking individuals in the organization will clear the way to have conversations with other high-ranking individuals. If the CEO can find the time to have this short meeting, then the other members of the senior team will be sure to find the time as well.

The CEO: The Beginning. If possible, the CEO would be the person to speak with first. If the CEO is not available, then beginning with another member of the senior management team would be the next best choice. The process should not be delayed because the meeting with the CEO is delayed.

Data-Gathering Mode. At this point in the process, the training professional is strictly in a data-gathering mode, not evaluating or judging the worthiness or accuracy of what the individuals say. The training professional should not respond with solutions, training or otherwise, to the reported problems. That is not the mission of the moment. The mission for now is to collect information on what these individuals think are the facilitators and barriers to the organization achieving its strategic goals. Gathering the information, writing it down immediately, and thanking the interviewee for sharing should be the training professional's only focus.

After conversations with the CEO, senior managers, and department managers, the next step is to collect information from supervisors. It is always desirable for the training professional to have one-on-one conversations with supervisors. If the organization is large, this may be a challenge due to the number of people in supervisory roles. If individual meetings are logistically difficult, the training professional can gather data from the supervisors through small-group meetings, staff meetings, surveys, or other convenient communication mechanisms.

Supervisors focus on their departmental goals and the people who report to them. Ask the supervisor, or group of supervisors:

1. What are the skills, knowledge, attitudes, and behaviors that support your staff members accomplishing their goals and
2. What are the barriers they face? Again, record the responses without evaluating, judging, or responding with any problem-solving or training-related strategies.

Data-Gathering Guidelines. The training professional must respect specific data gathering guidelines. The goal is an honest, forthright sharing of potentially sensitive information from people with significant organizational power. The training professional must protect the trusting relationship with the interviewee. To ensure trust, follow four key communication principles:

1. Tell the interviewees the reason for the meeting: to find out, from each person's perspective, the existing barriers to achieving the organization's goals. The training professional must tell the interviewee that the provided information will

be used to formulate training recommendations to address the needs discussed.

2. The training professional must also tell all interviewees about the complete data-gathering process. It is important to inform each interviewee, for example, that one-on-one interviews will be conducted with the CEO and all managers and that a survey will be sent to supervisors and non-supervisory employees. Also tell each interviewee that other sources of information will be reviewed (such as productivity reports, turnover statistics, performance evaluations, and health and safety records) so they know that this is a comprehensive data gathering process.

3. The interviewees must know that information collected in one-on-one interviews will be reported in trend form; no one individual's point of view will be revealed. Continue to honor this commitment of anonymity and confidentiality throughout the data-gathering process and submission of the results report to the decision-makers. The reputation and future of the training professional and the training effort depend on such discretion.

4. Inform the interviewees of the time frame for reporting results so they know when they can expect to hear recommendations and can plan accordingly. For instance, if the meetings are being conducted in the first quarter of the year (either fiscal or calendar), is it reasonable to expect to report the results in the second or third quarter? The training professional should anticipate, as best as possible, how long it will take to complete gathering data and writing the report. The following chapters of this book delineate the processes involved in organizing and ranking the collected information. That also gives the training professional an idea of the time necessary to adequately prepare recommendations

Gathering Information from Non-Supervisory Employees

Non-supervisory employees are an important information source for training needs. They have an interest in achieving their individual goals, their department achieving its goals, the organization achieving its strategic goals, and the company fulfilling its overall mission and purpose. Because of the number of people involved, this will be a difficult group for the training professional to meet with one-on-one or in group meetings. For the purpose of the training needs assessment process, the best way to receive information from this group is via survey.

Writing a Training Needs Assessment Survey. Rather than asking the question, "What, in your opinion, is supporting and/or getting in the way of achieving your individual goals?" it is more productive and informative to create a survey that lists a series of job-related skills, knowledge, and abilities and ask, "Which of these knowledge and/or skill areas, if enhanced, would have the greatest impact on your ability to achieve the goals of your job?" A rating scale next to each job-related knowledge/skill would measure responses ranging from low to high impact. The combined responses from all survey participants will enable the training professional to ascertain the knowledge and skills the respondents perceive have the lowest to highest impact on their ability to achieve their goals. The survey could look something like the one in Exhibit 3.1.

EXHIBIT 3.1.   TRAINING NEEDS ASSESSMENT SURVEY

The training department in your organization plans to offer training programs based on the needs identified by all members of the organization. This is your opportunity to help determine the direction and scope of future training programs. Please review the entire survey and once completed, return to the training department. Results will be distributed to the entire organization once the needs assessment process is completed. Thank you for your time and effort in completing this survey.
Regards,
[Training Manager Name and Signature]

Directions: Please review **each** of the skill/knowledge areas listed below. If **your skill/knowledge** were **enhanced in each** area, please indicate the **impact** you believe each would have on **your ability** to **achieve the goals of your job. Please place a checkmark in the appropriate space.**

A Practical Guide to Training and Development: Assess, Design, Deliver, and Evaluate. Copyright © 2008 by John Wiley & Sons, Inc. Reproduced by permission of Pfeiffer, an Imprint of Wiley. www.pfeiffer.com

(*Continued*)

EXHIBIT 3.1. *CONTINUED*

Knowledge/Skill	Low Impact	High Impact
Communication		
Computer		
Handling Conflict		
Culture and Diversity		
Customer Service		
Equipment Operation		
Health and Safety		
Dealing with Change		
Leading Effective Meetings		
Motivation		
Performance Evaluation		
Planning		
Policies and Procedures		
Presenting to Groups		
Problem Solving/Decision Making		
Product Knowledge		
Project Management		
Sales		
Selection Interviewing		
Sexual Harassment Prevention		
Team Effectiveness		
Time Management		
Total Quality Management		
Wellness		
Writing Skills		
Other		
Other		
Other		

Maximizing Survey Participation. Different structures and wording would need to be used, depending on whether this were a paper or electronic survey, but in either case, ensuring as close to 100 percent survey participation as possible is vitally important. Rewards for participating such as prizes or raffles work exceedingly well. Extremely high levels of survey participation, combined with the results of the management and supervisory interviews discussed previously, will give the training professional the raw information to determine the organization's most important training needs. If only a small percentage of non-supervisory employees complete the survey, significant data will be missed, and the ability to draw conclusions about training needs will be compromised.

Using Other Information Sources

In addition to conducting interviews and surveys, the training professional needs to explore other sources of organizational information to discover additional factors that prevent the organization from achieving its goals such as

- Customer satisfaction surveys and/or comment cards
- Employee performance appraisals
- Exit interview data trends
- Production reports
- Employee opinion surveys
- Workers' compensation reports
- Accident reports
- Employee assistance program utilization reports
- Lawsuits
- Audits
- Accreditation reports

Each of these data points might provide insight into potential facilitators and barriers to enterprise-wide strategic goals, departmental goals, and individual goals.

TASK ANALYSIS METHOD: A MICRO MODEL

Training's essential function is to facilitate change in employee knowledge, skills, attitudes, and behavior that supports the organization's mission and goal achievement. The task analysis model uses a step-by-step process that

1. Rates employee's level of ability to perform job tasks within a key result area;
2. Rates the necessity for each job task performed; and
3. Recommends an action plan that focuses on improving knowledge and skills so employees can more effectively perform essential job tasks within a key result area.

Other practices can be used to analyze employee task performance. Managers can observe employee behaviors in the field and use a checklist to note the knowledge and skills that need improvement. Tests can be administered to assess job knowledge. Reviewing past performance appraisals can uncover performance deficiencies in key result areas. According to this analysis and resulting training interventions, the goal is to improve individual job performance which leads to improved departmental goal achievement which will lead to improved enterprise-wide strategic goal achievement which will lead to a greater fulfillment of organization mission and purpose.

The job task analysis model fulfills several important functions:

- It is most appropriate to assist managers and/or supervisors and their direct reports in pinpointing knowledge/skill areas that are priority for training;
- It can assess future career development knowledge/skill needs and help prepare employees for their next job(s) within the organization;
- It can serve as a tool to develop an orientation program for new employees;
- It can help create course curricula for specific key result areas within specific job classifications, such as management, supervisory, customer service or sales; and
- As part of a performance appraisal process, it creates a priority list and action plan toward knowledge, skill and/or behavioral change and development in key result areas. And the process documents progress toward achieving desired changes.

Once the decision-makers decide to proceed with an organization-wide training initiative centered around a task analysis model, the process starts with a complete listing of job tasks for all classifications of employees.

Identifying Job Tasks

To identify training needs, a list of specific tasks necessary to perform a particular job needs to be generated. An up-to-date job description is ideal for this purpose as are descriptions of key result areas that contain performance standards as well as specific job tasks. If job task descriptions are not available, managers and their direct reports can develop this list together. Succinct statements (e.g., interview job applicants, prepare monthly financial statements), not detailed descriptions of job duties, are most desirable; the goal is to create an uncomplicated list of essential job tasks.

The job task list can be created in a number of different ways. The direct report may develop the list independently and submit it to the manager for review and additional input if necessary; the direct report and the manager may develop the list jointly; or the manager alone may develop the list. Which method to follow probably depends on the particular employee's job experience level. More experienced employees can create the list more independently; less experienced employees will need assistance from their managers.

All tasks for each key result area should be listed for each job classification. The appropriate number of job tasks varies depending on the complexity of the position. The correct number of tasks is the complete list of tasks. A large number of tasks may be perceived as overwhelming and potentially discouraging ("How can I possibly provide/receive training for all those skills?") for both managers and employees, and a significantly smaller number of statements may mean that important essential job tasks may be omitted. Both managers and their direct reports should put aside such concerns for now and focus on making sure that a complete list of job tasks for each key result area is in place.

Rating Levels of Ability and Task Necessity

The manager and direct report must now answer two questions related to each job task:

1. What is the present ability level of the employee for each? and
2. How necessary is adequate performance of the job task to meet position expectations?

The combined answers to these two questions will reveal either a discrepancy, indicating a training need or a match, indicating no change in knowledge and skill is necessary at this time. A sample form can be completed that allows for separate rating scales for levels of ability and task necessity for each job task within each key result area. As seen in Exhibit 3.2, the first space on the left of each continuum represents the lowest possible rating and the last space on the right of each continuum representing the highest possible rating.

Identifying Priority Training Needs

By examining the responses to questions 1 through 8 for each job task within each key result area, training needs become clearer. Job tasks where "level of ability" is rated low and "level of task necessity" is rated high indicate the most critical training needs. Job tasks where level of ability is rated low and level of task necessity is rated moderate indicate the next most critical training needs. Job tasks where level of ability is rated moderate and level of task necessity is rated high indicate the next most important training needs. Job tasks where level of ability is rated low or moderate and level of task necessity is rated low or moderate may indicate areas for future training and career development.

Completing the Training Action Plan

The Training Action Plan is a straightforward, brief document that summarizes the collected information and adds the elements of criticality, training activity, and timeframe for completion. Depending on the level of ability and level of task necessity as indicated in the previous section, the plan assigns a rating of (1) Critical Training Need; (2) Moderate Training Need; or (3) Future Training Opportunity to each job task. The plan then identifies training activities for each job task to provide the necessary change in knowledge, skills, attitudes, and behavior. Training activities may include internal programs, external programs, self-paced programs, or other sources of training discussed more

---

EXHIBIT 3.2.   RATING ABILITY AND TASK NECESSITY LEVELS

Key Result Area:

Task:

Rating Levels of Ability

Levels of ability are determined by filling in the appropriate space for each
   question for each job task. Manager and direct report must agree on
   each rating.

	1	2	3	4	5
1. How is the direct report viewed by others?	Novice				Expert
2. How much supervision is required?	Hands-On				Hands Off
3. What is the current level of expertise?	Low				High
4. How often are errors made?	Frequently				Infrequently

Rating Levels of Task Necessity

Levels of task necessity are determined by filling in the appropriate space for each
   question for each job task. Manager and direct report must agree on
   each rating.

	1	2	3	4	5
5. How often is the task performed?	Frequently				Infrequently
6. How important is the task to the whole job?	Essential				Not Essential
7. What impact do errors have on the organization?	Large				Small
8. What contribution does this task make to departmental and/or strategic organizational goals?	Significant				Insignificant

---

thoroughly in a future chapter. An estimated completion date, usually described in terms of quarters (Q1 = January to March; Q2 = April to June; Q3 = July to September; Q4 = October to December) pinpoints the commitment and increases the likelihood that both manager and employee will follow through.

Monitoring and Measuring Progress and Change

The manager should examine employee performance data on as many job tasks as possible before the employee engages in training activities. In this way, the manager can capture pre- and post-training levels of job task performance to demonstrate training's return on investment and contribution made to achieving the organization's goals.

The manager should also, with the employee's permission, place this training action plan in the employee's personnel file so it can be referred to in future one-on-one meetings. The plan is the written document that comes out of the analysis that serves as a timeline for training activities and their approximate completion dates. At least quarterly, the manager should monitor the progress of each employee's plan to ensure that the employee is meeting estimated completion dates and to provide encouragement.

If all managers complete their task analyses for each job classification they supervise and submit them to a central collection point, the organization can create a training matrix (described later in this chapter) for each job classification that identifies a program to enhance skills and knowledge for each job task. The training matrix serves as a program resource to improve knowledge and skill for any job in the organization.

Applying this process to a new employee whose ability levels are low in highly necessary tasks should provide the emphasis and a good portion of the agenda for new employee orientation training. It is the most frequently offered training program offered by organizations in the United States. It is a tremendous opportunity for new employees to learn knowledge, skills, attitudes, and behaviors deemed a priority and related to key job performance result areas. Imparted through training at the beginning of employment on both an enterprise-wide and departmental level, new employee orientation can serve as a positive and influential beginning of the employee's relationship with the organization's training efforts.

Examining Task Analysis: A Case Study

The (fictitious) manager of administrative services (Chris) must identify the training needs for the receptionists and administrative assistants who Chris supervises. The receptionists and administrative assistants support several managers at various locations throughout the organization. The manager will need to rate each receptionist and administrative assistant separately on their level of ability and level of task necessity in each key area.

Identifying Job Tasks. Chris prepares a list of job tasks performed by the receptionists and administrative assistants group under the key result area of "positive contact with others":

1. Meet and greet visitors
2. Answer phones
3. Take messages/direct messages to voice mail
4. Respond to e-mails
5. Prepare correspondence
6. Handle complaints
7. Document customer interaction using proprietary software

Rating Levels of Ability and Task Necessity. Chris is now ready to meet with the first employee (Pat) to rate Pat's ability level to perform each task and the criticality of each task. This part of the process could have been conducted separately by each party or by the manager, but Chris decides to do it in a meeting with Pat.

They first review the job task list under the key result area "positive contact with others" and decide that tasks 1 through 7 represent the most important elements. Then Chris says something to the effect of "Let's begin with your assessment of your current levels of ability to perform each task and your perception of the level of job necessity that each task represents. Be as honest as you can; this is not your performance evaluation. I will help as necessary by sharing my observations and experiences." They examine each of the seven job tasks, answering questions

1 through 8 from the rating form, then mutually agree on the rating for each question. Below is a summary of the results:

Job Task	Level of Ability	Level of Task Necessity
Meet/greet visitors	High	High
Answer phones	High	High
Take messages	High	High
Respond to e-mails	Moderate	Moderate
Handle complaints	High	High
Prepare correspondence	Low	Moderate
Use proprietary software	Low	High

Identifying Priority Training Needs. Based on rating levels of ability and task necessity, Chris and Pat agree on the most critical training needs, the tasks that are low in ability level and moderate to high in level of task necessity: preparing correspondence and using proprietary software.

Completing the Training Action Plan. The final step in the needs assessment process is for Chris and Pat to jointly complete the training action plan. Based on identified training needs and the fact that the discussion is taking place in the early stages of Q4, the training action plan would look like this:

Job Task	Training Activity	Est. Completion Date
Prepare correspondence	Writing Skills Workshop	Q1
Use proprietary software	Vendor Training Program	Q2

Extending the Process to Other Employees. Chris can now replicate this process through individual meetings with each of the administrative assistants and receptionists. Information on job tasks and rating levels of ability of task necessity would be tailored to the outcomes of the discussion with each employee as would the training action plan.

Monitoring and Measuring Progress and Change. Chris calendars and regularly checks in with each administrative assistant and receptionist to discuss progress (or lack thereof) toward completing the training action plan. It doesn't take very long to do and Chris feels it is a great use of time. Chris knows that the staff appreciates the interest, support, and attention; it has helped motivate them to complete their training plans. It's almost as if they would be letting Chris down if they fell short. Chris has also documented pre-training performance data for each job task that the administrative assistants and receptionists will receive training for so the contribution that training has made to achieving both departmental goals and the organization's strategic goals can be documented. For instance, Chris has documented that it took Pat an average of five drafts (equal to forty-five minutes) to prepare a letter. Pat also expressed exasperation and frustration at needing to produce so many multiple drafts to arrive at an acceptable document. After Pat attends the writing skills workshop during Q1, Chris will note how many fewer drafts (and less time) it will take to prepare an acceptable letter, along with the time savings and anecdotally reported reduced frustration.

NEEDS ASSESSMENT FREQUENCY

How often the needs assessment process should be repeated is a difficult question to answer. Conducting training needs assessments is an exhaustive, time-consuming, and expensive process that yields tremendously important data. The investment that the organization has made in the training effort is enormous, so it is important to focus training resources on priority needs. Annual assessments would be ideal, although conducting one every two or three years is probably adequate. Some of the factors that would drive the necessity to conduct training needs assessments more frequently are the following:

1. Changes in the industry (i.e., product and/or service technology);
2. Changes in employees (i.e., turnover); and
3. Changes in enterprise-wide strategic goal performance.

Any or all can determine the frequency with which a training needs assessment should be undertaken.

NEEDS ASSESSMENT RESULT TRENDS: A CASE STUDY

The professional literature has contained sparse information concerning the needs assessment processes organizations generally follow and the results they produce. An unpublished study by Moskowitz (2007) analyzed a large number of needs assessments conducted over several years to determine whether a trend existed in the results they produced.

Data Collection

From 1991 to 2006, 314 training needs assessments using the macro strategic goal model were conducted in companies throughout San Diego County. The organizations ranged in size from one hundred employees to several thousand. A wide variety of product/service providers were represented, including healthcare, manufacturing, biotech, pharmaceutical, nonprofit, real estate, temp. agencies, insurance, government, banking, retail, aerospace, travel and leisure, computer hardware and software, telecommunications, engineering, and utilities.

Data Analysis

A total of 211 different topic areas were uncovered, grouped into forty-nine standard topic areas. Frequency of mention was tabulated for the topic areas, as seen in Figure 3.1.

Results

The twelve topics listed below were most frequently mentioned in the 314 assessments and were ranked as either a first or second priority, as indicated:

Training Topic	Frequency of Mention	Ranked Number 1	Ranked Number 2
1. Communication	131	36	32
2. Product Knowledge	109	28	33
3. Customer Service	99	37	21
4. Leadership and Management	88	20	20

5. Computer Skills	79	21	10
6. Team Building	76	11	24
7. Performance Appraisal	74	19	5
8. Health and Safety	68	22	12
9. Coaching and Counseling	62	14	5
10. Time Management/ Delegation	60	10	6
11. Selection Interviewing	49	20	10
12. Sales	40	7	13

Discussion

Because the existing literature on training needs assessment results is sparse, it is difficult to compare the results of this fifteen-year longitudinal study with any other study. It appears to be the most complete effort to date to determine whether a commonality of training needs exists across organizations, regardless of their size or industry type. The results of this study are clear: A cluster of specific knowledge and skill areas, led by communication training, are viewed as training priorities and have consistently been viewed this way for the past fifteen years.

The reasons for this finding are interesting to explore. It could be that this cluster of knowledge and skills has consistently ranked highest because these capabilities are viewed as most important to accomplishing the organizations goals. It seems intuitive that enhancing employee knowledge and skills associated with these top-ranked topics would contribute to the organization's success.

Additionally, perhaps these are the knowledge and skill sets that continually rank high in need because ongoing and rapidly changing technology requires immediate and continuous knowledge and skills updating, especially product knowledge and computer skills. These are also the knowledge and skills areas that

| | Prioritized Topic Occurrence Frequency | | | | | | | | | | | | | | | | | | | |
	1	2	3	4	5	6	7	8	9	10	11	12	13	14	15	16	17	18	19	Total
Career Development	3	4	7	2	1		2					1								**20**
Coaching/ Counseling	14	5	13	7	9	3	2	4	2	2			1							**62**
Communication Skills	36	32	19	25	8	4	2	1	1	1	2	1								**131**
Compensation and Benefits	6	6	1	4		3		1	1		1		1							**24**
Computer Skills	21	10	13	18	4	2	4	2	1	2	2									**79**
Conflict Management	5	4	7	3	7	3	1	1	1	1	1									**33**
Contract Administration		1	1				1	1												**4**
Creativity											1	1								**2**
Cross Training	5	3	3	3	3		1	1												**19**
Culture and Diversity	7	3	7	3	3		1		2				1	1						**28**
Customer Service	37	21	21	5	4	1	1	2	2	1	1	1	1	1	1					**99**

(*Continued*)

FIGURE 3.1. (Continued)

Prioritized Topic Occurrence Frequency

	1	2	3	4	5	6	7	8	9	10	11	12	13	14	15	16	17	18	19	Total
Employment Law	3	7	5	4	2	2	2			1										**26**
Equipment		1	2	1	2		1													**7**
ESL	1				2	1			1											**5**
Ethics			1		1	1				1	2									**6**
Finance	2	4	3	1	1	1	1	1			1		1	1	1					**17**
Foreign Language	1			1																**2**
Health and Safety	22	12	8	7	7	4	1	2	1	1				2			1			**68**
Health and Wellness	4	5	5	5	4	3	1	1	1				1							**29**
Laws and Regulations	1	1	1	1	1	1	1													**6**
Leadership and Management Skills	20	20	19	8	10	1	1	2	2	1	1		1	1	1					**88**
Managing Change	4	5	6		2	3		3	1	1										**25**
Marketing	3		1	1	1															**6**
Material Management								1												**1**
Meetings Management	3	2	1	3	1	1	1	1	1	1	1			1						**16**

														Total
Motivation	8	3	5	3	6	1	2	1			1		1	**31**
Negotiation	3	1	2	1		1								**8**
New Employee Orientation	13	5	6	4	1	2	2	1	1		2			**37**
On-the-Job Training	2	3	1	1	1									**8**
Performance Appraisal	19	15	12	5	5	3	6	3	3	1	2			**74**
Performance Standards	3	3	2	1										**9**
Planning	7	6	8	5	2	3	1	1	1		1			**35**
Policies and Procedures	6	8	6	5	5	2	1	1	1	1	1			**37**
Presentation Skills	1	4	3	2	2	3	1	1	1	1	1			**20**
Problem Solving and Decision Making	2	8	5	5	3	2	1	1	1	1				**29**
Product Knowledge	28	33	17	6	4	5	2	4	1	2	2	1	1	**109**
Project Management	4	6	5	2	2	1	1	1	1					**21**

(Continued)

FIGURE 3.1. (Continued)

Prioritized Topic Occurrence Frequency

	1	2	3	4	5	6	7	8	9	10	11	12	13	14	15	16	17	18	19	Total
Recruitment and Retention	9	4	8		1	3				1										26
Sales	7	13	7	4	3	2	1	1	1	1										40
Selection	20	10	5	2	6	1	1	1	1			1	1							49
Interviewing																				
Sexual Harassment	7	3	4	2	4	3	1		1							1				26
Supervisory Skills	12	9	3	2	2	1	4												1	34
Team Building	11	24	12	10	4	8	4	1	1					1						76
Time	10	6	8	15	12	1	4	1		1		1		1						60
Management and Delegation																				
TQM	8	8	4	5	2	2	1	1	1				1							33
Train the Trainer	2	1		2	1	2												1		9
Violence in the Workplace		3														1				4
Writing Skills	1	1	4	2		2		2							1					13
Other	2	5	2	2	2		4			1										18

affect all the organization's employees, so the training need is pronounced throughout the ranks.

The specific reasons these knowledge and skill sets consistently rose to the top of the training need list over the fifteen year study are open to speculation and further investigation. It seems safe to say that regardless of the reasons, organizations would serve their vision and mission by enhancing employee capabilities in these and other areas that rank high in training needs assessment results.

RESISTANCE TO THE NEEDS ASSESSMENT PROCESS

Organizations report the training topics they provide to their employees. However, there seems to be a lack of information available in the literature regarding training needs assessment results. It is difficult to determine the reasons for this finding. It's possible that assessments are being frequently conducted and results not reported because of organizational reluctance to reveal sensitive information. Conversely, it's possible that assessments are not being done very frequently.

If the latter is true, there are several potential reasons that organizations may not be initiating a training need assessment process;

- A lack of senior management's willingness to examine the organization's training needs
- A lack of expertise in how to conduct a needs assessment
- A lack of perceived need to initiate a needs assessment process (comfort with the status quo)
- A lack of available resources to focus on a needs assessment
- An abundance of training resources so there is no perceived urgency to prioritize needs and initiate an assessment process
- The belief that training already focuses on perceived needs so collecting validating data is not necessary

The organization's senior management team must collectively decide to initiate a training needs assessment process before any such efforts will occur. They need to perceive the value of identifying, prioritizing, and addressing training needs before the assessment effort can be launched.

USING NEEDS ASSESSMENT RESULTS

Lack of teamwork. Communication gaps. Inability to manage conflict. Unclear job description and performance goals. Resistance to change. Product knowledge deficiencies. Slow to market. Bad hiring decisions. Unwarranted terminations. Poorly executed performance evaluations. Not addressing good or bad work performance. Not customer friendly. Allegations of sexual harassment. High turnover rates. Staffing deficiencies. Compensation inequities. Computer problems. Policy and procedure issues.

Common issues that normally surface during the training needs assessment process are all serious and potentially fatal to the organization's ability to fulfill its vision and mission and achieve its enterprise-wide strategic goals. Some or all of the issues may need immediate attention. Challenge number one, after completing the needs assessment process, is to review all of the information gathered and decide how to categorize, rank and address the issues appropriately. Categorizing must precede ranking.

CATEGORIZING RESULTS: TRAINING OR NON-TRAINING ISSUES

In this context, to categorize means to differentiate barriers to goal achievement that can most likely be remedied via training from barriers to goal achievement when a different problem-solving approach is more appropriate. Not all issues raised in the needs assessment can or should require a training program. By noting and addressing non-training-related issues separately in the needs assessment report to the decision makers, the training professional is forwarding important data to the appropriate management people for review. While not an exhaustive treatment, listed below are some of the frequently mentioned training and non-training-related issues uncovered during a needs assessment.

Motivation. Employees who lack motivation are stating that they feel no reason (motive) to meet or exceed performance expectations. Management must deal with this problem effectively or not achieve organizational goals. Problems could have originated from a variety of potential sources that the employees perceive negatively: leadership and/or management styles, compensation and benefits, incentives, performance management, and/or staffing. Management must address motivation-related issues to fulfill the organization's vision and mission.

Leadership and Management. On an ongoing basis, leaders and managers influence the activities of individuals and groups to achieve organizational goals in given situations. Knowledge, skills, attitudes, and behaviors are required to effectively perform this role on a daily basis. Deficiencies in this competency will have far ranging negative consequences throughout the organization. Interventions, including training, have the potential for improving leader and manager competencies.

Compensation, Benefits, and Incentives. Employees must believe their compensation, benefits, and incentive packages are fair or their job performance levels may be depressed. Fairness is an extremely subjective and difficult concept to define. Fairness appears to be present when compensation, benefits, and incentive comparisons with organizations of similar size, product/service, and geographic location show minimal differences. Compensation and benefits survey data can determine whether a gap exists and needs to be addressed.

Performance Management Systems. Performance management systems, those structures in the organization that influence job performance, can serve to either help or hinder employee goal achievement. Mechanisms must be in place that measure and monitor individual performance. Action must be taken on a consistent and continual basis to reward positive performance and address negative performance. Future goals must be established and communicated to achieve retention and career development.

Staffing. Too much work to do with too few employees, over an extended time period, diminishes individual job performance and results in burnout, disability, and turnover. Too many employees also diminishes individual job performance and causes an inordinate salary expense that lessens the organization's ability to achieve its financial goals. Organizations need to calculate the correct number of people in each job classification to adequately handle the workload flexibly to deal with cyclical increases and decreases in business volume. Hiring and retention processes must maintain the proper employee number per job classification.

Policies and Procedures. If there is a lack of complete, accurate, and up-to-date operational policies and procedures for executing particular processes, recommend creating and/or rewriting policies and procedures so they are complete and up-to-date. If the issues revolve around human resource policies and procedures, recommend creating and disseminating an employee handbook. Alternatively, if the issue is that the policies and procedures are fine, but people don't know about or follow them, then informing them through training would be the appropriate remedy. The change that needs to occur is different depending on the true source of the problem.

Facilities. A variety of facilities-related issues may prevent goal achievement. Perhaps cramped work areas inhibit performance. Insufficient parking and/or lack of access to the worksite via mass transit may cause a problem. Heating and/or air conditioning malfunctions may make working conditions less pleasant. Food service limitations, such as a lack of adequate eating facilities, may be identified. Perhaps the neighborhood in which the worksite is located is perceived as unsafe so people are concerned about their personal health and safety. No amount of training can correct these infrastructure problems. But just because training cannot correct them doesn't mean they should be ignored. They should be included as findings in the needs assessment report and discussed by senior management.

Equipment. Equipment issues, be they manufacturing/production, computer/Internet, or telecommunication-related, may prevent employees and the organization from achieving goals. Obsolete equipment may be slow, may break down more often, and be more costly to maintain and repair than the latest model. Old and slow computers operating outdated software present all sorts of problems. Telecommunication infrastructure deficiencies can affect many business processes and greatly inhibit an organization's competitive edge. No amount of training can update equipment or computers. These are issues, if identified, that need to be reported and addressed by senior management.

If, however, the issue is that the existing equipment is fine, but that employees don't know how to operate it efficiently and/ or safely without breaking it or injuring themselves, then it is more likely that training can address/solve the problem directly. Similarly, if software is up-to-date, but employees don't know how to use it, then training may solve that problem as well.

RANKING RESULTS

The list of training needs that are identified through a comprehensive assessment process is daunting. The training professional cannot deal with all of them simultaneously. A process must be created to prioritize items so that the most pressing needs, those that have the greatest impact on the enterprise-wide organizational goals, are addressed first.

Overcoming Ranking Difficulties. Categorize the original list of needs to reduce the list. Include only those that training can address through improving employee knowledge, skills, attitudes, and behavior. Then the training professional must rank the list. Ranking is not an easy task considering the breadth of the issues identified. Most, if not all, of the issues raised in the needs assessment appear important. Most, if not all, seem to require some level of immediate attention. Most, if not all, appear to lead to dire circumstances if they are not immediately addressed.

Understanding Ranking Requirements. Ranking is required because it will be impractical (if not impossible) to facilitate knowledge, skills, attitude, and behavior change to address each issue simultaneously. Time and resource limits are important considerations. Too much change in a short period of time can cause unnecessary upheaval and discomfort. The training professional must determine priorities before beginning the change process.

The training professional's ultimate goal is to initiate improvements to employee knowledge, skills, attitudes, and behaviors that will have the greatest positive impact on the organization's strategic goals. The professional's gut feeling may point to topic A, that changes in people's behavior related to topic A will have a great impact on the organization's strategic goals. But as the saying goes: "In God we trust; everyone else bring data." The training professional must provide supporting documentation to the decision-makers who will approve the training initiative.

Using a Selection Grid. Many processes can be used that assist in making a subjective process more objective. Applying a process called a selection grid is useful for ranking items based on established criteria. A selection grid is an excellent method for ranking the list of training topics that the needs assessment process generated. See Figure 3.2 for an example.

The spreadsheet lists each topic area in a column down the left-hand side, and the organization's enterprise-wide strategic goals are listed across the top. Using the same 1 to 5 scale, the

FIGURE 3.2. SELECTION GRID FOR PRIORITIZING TRAINING PROJECTS

| | | Strategic Goals | | | | |
		Customer Satisfaction	Sales	Employee Satisfaction	Net Profit	Total
	Communication	5	5	4	3	17
	Computer Skills	5	3	3	3	14
	Conflict Management	5	2	4	2	13
	Customer Service	5	5	3	4	17
Training Topic	Leadership/ Management	3	3	5	3	14
	Managing Change	4	3	4	2	13
	Product Knowledge	5	5	3	5	18
	Team Building	2	3	5	3	13
	Sales	4	5	2	4	15
	Time Management	2	3	3	3	11
	Writing Skills	2	2	2	2	8

impact of the anticipated knowledge/skill/attitude/behavior improvement represented by each training topic on each organizational strategic goal is noted in each cell. Summing the total score for each training topic will reveal the knowledge or skill changes that will have the greatest potential impact. Approximately 5 to 10 percent of the topics will yield the highest scores, 80 to 90 percent of the topics will score in the middle of the range, and 5 to 10 percent of the topics will score at the low end of the continuum. The training professional should recommend the topics with the highest scores to the decision-makers as training priorities for the organization. Each topic had appeared important before the selection grid process. After completing the process, it is apparent from the selection grid that training in product knowledge, communication, and customer service that would have the greatest impact on the organization's strategic goals.

Solo or Group Process. The selection grid is the basis for training recommendations to the organization's decision-makers. The training professional can undertake the selection grid process alone. If, however, the professional's sole opinion is not sufficient, then a team approach is warranted. Involve as many decision-makers as possible in rating the grid cells. Then the decision-makers are more likely to buy into the process and resulting selection grid.

After the arduous process of identifying and organizing training needs data has been completed, the training professional is ready to begin designing training. The many important considerations and decisions that affect this part of the process will begin to be discussed in the next chapter.

Summary

1. Organizations make a sizable financial investment in training and development to support their vision and mission.

2. Organizations need to embark on a training needs identification and prioritization process to focus training resources on the most urgent knowledge and skill development issues.

3. The assessment process needs to involve data collection from all organizational levels as well as from reports and other data sources.

4. A case study involving 314 completed training needs assessments indicated that a cluster of training topics appears to continually rank highest.

5. Non-training organizational issues raised by the needs assessments process need to be addressed by management.

6. A selection grid is a useful tool to prioritize training needs.

CHAPTER FOUR

TRAINING DESIGN

"Everyone thinks of changing the world, but no one thinks of changing himself."
LEO TOLSTOY

PURPOSE

This chapter will enable you to accomplish the following:

- Identify the main precepts of adult learning theory
- Recognize the important role that adult learning theory plays in training design
- Create a program plan that identifies specific design requirements and constraints
- Design goal statements that clarify program outcomes
- Develop a training budget

OVERVIEW

Once the organization's training needs have been identified through the assessment process, many factors must be considered in order to create a training experience that successfully changes employee knowledge, skills, attitudes, and behaviors. Creating and/or maintaining a supportive educational environment that incorporates adult learning theory is essential. The training professional must:

1. Determine and fulfill specific training design features including requirements and constraints

2. Decide on a training medium (classroom led instruction, e-learning, or blended learning
3. Establish and follow budget guidelines
4. Gain management support
5. Market training to the organization

This chapter also suggests a process for identifying specific and measurable knowledge and/or skill improvement goals that specifically describe training outcomes.

Adult Learning Theory: Malcolm Knowles

Winston Churchill said, "Personally, I'm always ready to learn, although I do not always like being taught!" Employees are at different stages in their readiness to learn as well as their receptivity to being taught. The trainer role is responsible to ensure that both learning (change) and teaching (training) takes place so that the changes indicated in the needs assessment are addressed. The organization's learning culture, along with interplay between training program design, trainer behavior, and participant predisposition, play key roles in influencing the environment so that it best supports adult learning.

Malcolm Knowles (1913–1997) is considered the central figure in U.S. adult education in the second half of the 20th century. He was the first to chart the rise of the adult education movement in the United States, to develop a statement of informal adult education practice, and to develop a comprehensive theory of adult education termed *andragogy,* characteristics of adult learners and how they learn that are different from characteristics and assumptions about how children learn. He championed the concept of self-directed learning, a process in which individuals take the initiative to diagnose their learning needs, formulate learning goals, identify resources, choose and implement learning strategies, and evaluate outcomes. He authored over 230 articles and eighteen books. Knowles was born in Montana, the son of a veterinarian. He earned a scholarship and received a B.A. degree from Harvard, as well as an M.A. and Ph.D. from the University of Chicago. During his graduate studies, he came in contact with and was influenced by the work of renown psychologists Carl Rogers and Kurt Lewin.

In 1959, Knowles was appointed to the faculty of Boston University as associate professor of adult education. In 1974, he joined the faculty of the Department of Education at North Carolina State University, where he remained until his retirement.

ANDRAGOGY

For Knowles, andragogy was built on the premise of four (he later added a fifth) essential assumptions about adult learners that differentiated them from child learners. Until this point, adult learning had been based on pedagogy (the ways children learn), but Knowles sought to establish a separate and different set of precepts to guide the learning process for adults.

MATURITY

Knowles used the concept of maturity to differentiate learners— those who are more "adult-like" and therefore more likely to take responsibility for their learning and those who are more "child-like" and therefore more likely to allow others to take the learning responsibility for them. The concept of maturity is not purely age-related in the sense that older workers are considered more mature than younger workers, nor is it generalized or reported to be reflected in a physical, psychological, social, or emotional sense. Rather, maturity depends on several factors.

a. *Self-Concept.* As people mature, their self-concepts change from being dependent to one that is self-directed.
b. *Experience.* As people mature, they accumulate a growing reservoir of experience that becomes a resource for learning.
c. *Readiness to Learn.* As people mature, their readiness to learn becomes oriented increasingly to the development of social roles.
d. *Orientation to Learning.* As people mature, their time perspectives change from one of postponed knowledge application to immediate knowledge application; accordingly, their orientation toward learning shifts from a subject focus to a problem-solving focus.
e. *Motivation to Learn.* As people mature, their motivation to learn shifts from being externally driven to being internally driven.

Self-Direction

Knowles described self-direction, as it relates to learning, as an ongoing process in which individuals, with or without the assistance of others, diagnose needs, formulate goals, identify resources, choose strategies, implement activity, and evaluate outcomes. In essence, he advocates that individuals conduct their own learning needs assessments and access resources (training) to assist with changes in knowledge, skills, attitudes, and behaviors. Knowles postulated that being self-directed (as opposed to being directed by others) has three distinct advantages that proactive learners have over passive learners;

1. They are more purposeful, more highly motivated, and tend to retain and make better use of the knowledge and skills they have learned;
2. They are more in-tune with our natural processes to want to take increasingly greater responsibility for our own lives; and
3. New developments in educational theory put a great deal more emphasis on learners taking responsibility for their own learning. Many organizations have adopted this position, so students entering organizations without this orientation will be at a disadvantage and will experience anxiety, frustration, and often failure as will their teachers.

Trainer Challenges and Strategies for Incorporating Adult Learning Concepts

Employees in the role of adult learners/training participants are at vastly different maturity stages related to each of the five andragogy precepts. Yet the successful trainer must design training to effectively facilitate change in knowledge, skills, attitudes, and behavior with all members of this diverse adult learner population.

Some common challenges and strategies to facilitating change are discussed below. The training professional should closely examine their own organization, with its unique set of circumstances, and design training so that adult learning principles are integrated into the fabric of the training effort. Many of these actions occur long before the adult learner steps foot in a classroom (virtual or otherwise) or begins an e-learning experience.

SELF-CONCEPT

Employees with more dependent personalities will be more likely to look to the trainer for guidance and direction. Their movement from denial and resistance to exploration and commitment may be more rapid and not require as much of a rationale and supporting information as employees who are more self-directed. Those who are less self-directed may also be less likely to self-manage progress through e-learning modules.

Employees with more self-directed personalities will be more likely to rely on their own instincts to decide whether to change. The trainer will probably need to provide supporting data that justifies the need to change. Needs assessment results will help. These employees, if they buy into the process, will probably be more willing and able to self-manage through an e-learning program than a less mature employee.

EXPERIENCE

Less mature or experienced employees will be more likely to be influenced to change their behavior by looking to the wisdom and advice of the trainer than more mature or experienced employees. In classroom training, the trainer must establish credibility and impart knowledge as well as facilitate the sharing of information by the more experienced employees through discussion. In this setting, more mature employees will feel and express frustration, resentment, and even anger if their relevant experience is not recognized by the trainer.

READINESS TO LEARN

Employees who are more mature perceive themselves as being more responsible for their own lives and proactive in their attempts to acquire additional knowledge and skill. In a November 13, 2007, article by the *Evening Gazette* (UK), Judd talks about the outcomes of a local conference, saying: "Encouraging skills development in the workplace presently has become a more open discourse, as [fewer] employees are reluctant to acknowledge their need for assistance." They will set high standards for the trainer, anticipating that the trainer will have knowledge to share and the expertise to teach it. Mature learners will expect to be treated as active participants in the training experience. In some instances, posing the question to participants of WIIFM to embrace this change as a training activity at the beginning of the session will bring readiness-to-learn factors to the surface and also give the training professional the opportunity to hear and respond to statements that suggest denial and resistance to change.

This can create a challenge for some trainers, who too often view adult learners as passive, dependent individuals sitting back with folded arms saying, "Teach me!" The training professional must correct this erroneous perception and prepare to be challenged by ready-to-learn adults.

Orientation to Learning

More mature employees are in knowledge-application mode more so than less mature employees, who are still in knowledge-acquisition mode. For the more mature training participant, answers to the question "What's in it for me?" are of paramount importance and serve to encourage an orientation-to-learn attitude that facilitates behavior change. Explicit rewards such as improved chances for lateral and/or promotional job opportunities, perquisites, and/or merit and/or bonus salary adjustments may motivate them. Implicit rewards like learning new skills to make the job easier, more interesting and/or challenging and to make the employee feel good are other forces that may reward and create an orientation to learn.

Clarification of Expectations

Mature adult learners become more ready to learn (and change) when they know and understand what is expected of them as a training outcome. Review training goal statements (discussed later in this chapter) at the beginning of the training session to clarify expected outcomes for training participants and enhance learner readiness to explore the proposed change.

First Impressions

First impressions of the training experience significantly affect adult learners, regardless of their maturity levels. The initial impact of the first five minutes will tend to remain throughout the training session. If what happens in the first five minutes is received positively, the session will tend to remain positive. If what happens in the first five minutes is received negatively, the training experience may not achieve its desired outcomes. Regardless of the training medium (to be discussed later in this chapter) the trainee's initial impression must be positive for a potentially productive learning experience.

In instructor-led classroom training, the trainer does not have a second chance to make a first impression. Great care must be taken to plan the first few, critical moments of the training program. At the most basic and immediate level, most adult learners want to know that the training professional is competent, knowledgeable, and enthusiastic about the topic. Chapter 5 will explore the subject of training delivery.

When asked, many trainees can quickly recall a bad training experience. They confirm that, when the first impression is negative, the downhill spiral is hard to stop. In instructor-led classroom training, a negative first impression will damage the presenter's credibility—participants will doubt the presenter's ability and knowledge—so participants will be less likely to embrace the training experience. Starting the session with a joke (that people don't find funny), or an off-the-subject story, a long drawn-out participant introduction exercise, or talking negatively about the training topic ("I know this is a boring subject, but. . . . ") waste valuable time and undermine the ability to achieve the training program's goals by the end of the session.

Practice Time

Employees of both high and low maturity levels generally appreciate time within the training session to practice new skills and behaviors. The cliché that "practice makes perfect" really translates, in training terms, to practice facilitates change. Perfection really doesn't exist except in the minds of perfectionists! Participants with both high and low maturity levels benefit from the opportunity to practice the new skills and behaviors in a safe, supportive learning environment. Practicing during training makes it more likely that the participant will bring the new behaviors to the workplace.

For example, providing practice writing sample performance evaluation narratives, counseling memos, and standards of work performance are very useful learning activities that facilitate behavior change. Computer training that allows participants to practice creating sample documents and manipulate data while working with various software programs gives the trainee the confidence to apply the new knowledge back at work. Just as physical exercise gives the human body muscle and brain memory for future use, training exercise gives the participant physiological and psychological memory for future use.

Practice also provides opportunities to demonstrate whether or not a desired training result has been achieved. For instance, if a goal is that "by the end of the training session, a minimum of 90 percent of the participants will be able to create a slide with five bullet points using PowerPoint," the statement can include "as demonstrated by the creation of said document during the training program." The practice session now serves the dual purpose of giving the participants the opportunity to explore the new behavior as well as finding out if the desired training program result has been achieved

PROGRAM DESIGN PLAN

A program design plan guides the trainer to ask (and answer) specific questions about the training program.

1. What are the goals of the training program?
2. How will success be measured?
3. What are the key topics that must be covered?
4. In what sequence will the topics be presented?
5. What training medium(s) will be used?

6. Considering the organization's environment and culture, what are the program's requirements and constraints?

Program design decisions are intended to support trainers and adult learners in their mutual quest to facilitate change in knowledge, skills, attitudes, and behaviors to improve work performance and contribute to goal achievement.

Start at the End: Create SMART Goals

A favored approach is to begin training design by determining the desired results. Desired results should be determined by addressing the necessary changes in knowledge, skills, attitudes, and behaviors the needs assessment revealed.

Robert Mager, in his seminal book *Preparing Instructional Objectives* (1962), states that before preparing instruction, before choosing material or method, it is vitally important to state goals clearly. Completing the statement "By the end of the training program participants will be able to . . . " with three, four, or, at the most, five desired behavioral results become the training program's goals. Stating the desired behavioral results in SMART terms—specific, measurable, attainable, role-related, time-bound—helps ensure that trainer and participant have a common understanding of the desired training outcomes.

For example, if the training program for the target audience aims to increase their product knowledge, one typical SMART goal statement might be "By the end of the training program, 95 percent of the participants will demonstrate a higher knowledge level of the organization's products and/or services, as measured by their achieving a higher score on a post-program questionnaire as compared to a pre-program questionnaire." To assess successful completion of this goal, product knowledge questionnaires would be completed by all training participants both before and after the training program. Successful completion of this goal would be realized if 95 percent of the participants achieved a higher score on the post-training questionnaire, as compared to the pre-training questionnaire.

Once the trainer has identified goal statements and communicated them to participants, every moment of the training program must focus on learning activities to help the participants achieve these goals.

Specificity. Goal specificity means avoiding terms open to a wide range of interpretation. Consider the following examples:

Terms Open to Many Interpretations	Terms Open to Fewer Interpretations
to know	to write
to understand	to recite
to really understand	to identify
to appreciate	to differentiate
to fully appreciate	to solve
to grasp the significance of	to construct
to enjoy	to list
to believe	to compare
to feel	to demonstrate

Stating goals that are open to fewer interpretations increases the chances that participants will achieve the training program's expectations.

Measurability. Goal achievement can also be measured by observing and comparing pre- and post-training program behavior. For example, another goal of the product knowledge training program for the target audience might be that "By the end of the training program, 95 percent of the participants will demonstrate a higher knowledge level of the organization's products and/or services, as measured by the supervisor's observations of the participant's discussions with customers." Supervisors could observe trainees and complete a behavioral checklist both pre and post training to document changes in product knowledge behavior.

Goal achievement can also be measured by documenting and comparing pre- and post-training program job performance results. For example, another goal of the product knowledge training program for the target audience might be that "By the end of the training program, 95 percent of the participants will demonstrate higher levels of job performance results as measured by a 5 percent increase in key result areas such as . . . " which would be determined by the employee's role in the organization.

Attainability. The trainer must be confident that the goal is attainable so as not to frustrate him- or herself as well as the participants. Unrealistic goals serve no useful purpose. The example used previously of 95 percent of participants gaining additional product knowledge may be unrealistic to the trainer.

Conversely, goals set too low do not serve to motivate the trainer or participants to achieve changes to their capability levels. The organization, having invested in the training effort and expecting a return in the form of changed behavior, may feel it is not getting its money's worth if the targeted outcome is set too low. If, for example, the target for the product knowledge training cited previously stated that the goal was for 50 percent of the participants to demonstrate greater knowledge, the organization might not feel that the training was yielding an adequate return on investment.

Role-Related. The training goal must be related to the participant's role in the organization; it must be relevant and worth striving for. For example, the goal of product knowledge training that "By the end of the training program, 95 percent of the participants will demonstrate a higher knowledge level of the organization's products and/or services, as measured by the supervisor's observations of the participant's discussions with customers" is very relevant if the participants job duties include interaction with customers. The goal is irrelevant for employees whose job duties include no interaction with customers.

Time-Bound. Goals need to be time-bound. Many would say a goal is not a goal without a timing element. Success in achieving training goals can be determined by stating that changes have to be observed by the end of the training program. Goals can also be constructed so that changes in learning, behavior, and/ or results can be measured at certain milestones after the training has been completed to determine whether new skills have maintained. Citing the previous example, a training goal might be stated that "By the end of the training program, 95 percent of the participants will demonstrate a higher knowledge level of the organization's products and/or services, as measured by their achieving a higher score on a post-program questionnaire administered two months after completing training as compared to a questionnaire administered prior to training."

Be SMART or Get Lost. Any training goal worth achieving can be written in SMART terms. If the training professional cannot create a training goal in SMART terms, then the trainer should question the value of striving to achieve that goal. Without a SMART goal, the trainer will not know whether the goal was achieved, since the measurement does not exist. Nor will the trainer be able to communicate the desired result clearly to the trainees. If the training goal cannot be written in SMART terms, it should not be part of the training program.

Using Goal Statements to Advantage

Constructing and communicating end-of-training goal statements has many other significant benefits. Sharing them with the adult learners at the beginning of the training session, along with the agenda, clarifies and focuses the direction of the training session for the program participants. Most training topics can vary widely in scope and content (think of all the directions a training program on communication, product knowledge, or leadership can take) so presenting training goals at the beginning of the session helps participants identify the specific areas of the broad topic that will and will not be covered.

As mentioned previously, goal statements are the foundation for evaluating training success once the program is completed. Goal statements serve as the metrics to measure the outcomes of programs, to quantify the return on investment of knowledge, skill, attitudinal and/or behavioral changes that have occurred.

Also, as mentioned previously, not all changes will occur and be measurable at the conclusion of the training program. Some changes can only be measured once the participant returns to work and performs the applicable task. Tell training participants if some evaluation aspects will be measured after the training has occurred.

Apply the Rule of Exception

SMART goals, to be attainable, should not be written in absolute terms. Goal statements that use terms such as "always" or "never" to describe outcomes are almost certain to fail. Invoke the 5 percent rule, which applies to practically all groups of trainees. The

5 percent rule suggests that a small segment of the trainee population, usually one out of twenty, moves to the beat of a different drum. (They are not with the program!) Therefore, the 5 percent rule should be accounted for in the metrics that the training professional creates for the program. For example, if the goal is to improve trainee scores on a pre- to post-training instrument, then assume that, at best, 95 percent of the trainees' scores will improve. Count on one out of twenty to have his or her score stay the same or drop. Anecdotal trainer experience reinforces that this rule of exception seems to occur over and over again. If the trainer is able to achieve a positive change in knowledge, skills, attitude, and/or behavior with 95 percent of the participants, the trainer should consider him- or herself highly successful.

Training goals also help identify the key topics that should be covered to address concerns raised in the needs assessment.

COVER KEY TOPICS

Key topics to cover in training can come from a variety of information sources: needs assessment results, customer feedback, performance evaluations, exit interview data, best-practices information, literature reviews, product vendors, and subject-matter experts can all be potential sources that help determine important training topics. For example, key topics for product knowledge training might include important customer conveniences, durability characteristics, manufacturing specifications, quality features, troubleshooting problems, frequently asked questions, warranty information, price, built-in safety protections, and repair and return policies

The number of key topics often exceeds the time allotted for training. The trainer must then decide:

1. Request additional training time;
2. Break the session into multiple meetings; or
3. Prioritize the key topics and only include the most essential.

MANAGE TRAINING TIME

Once the training professional has established training program goals and the key topics to cover, the trainer's mission is to spend every moment in the training session focused on achieving those results. Training time must be managed effectively and efficiently to succeed. Results aren't easy to attain because participants are at all stages of the maturity continuum. Overcoming denial and resistance and moving people to exploration and commitment to new knowledge, skills, attitudes, and behaviors will be very difficult to achieve. Training time management is the same as job time management. Employee A who identifies and focuses on job priorities and goals to achieve the desired results by the end of the workday equates to Trainer A who identifies and focuses on training program priorities and goals to achieve the desired results by the end of the training program.

Sequence Topics

The trainer determines topic sequence if, conceptually, it will be most effective to generate information from broad concepts to specific details or from specific details to broad topics. Visualize a funnel. If a funnel is upright, the large opening is at the top, and the small opening is at the bottom. The training program can begin with a broad treatment of the topic and then slowly but surely get more and more specific. Or the approach can more approximate the pattern of an inverted funnel, where training begins with very specific details about the topic and then broadens to the more conceptual as the training session progresses. Or, perhaps, there is more of a straight progression, or tunnel, where information is presented in a more linear manner.

The training professional must decide the most effective approach given the specific material. Mitchell (1987) advocates using yet another method, the spool pattern. Visualize two funnels connected by their spouts, creating a spool. Mitchell advocates beginning the training on a conceptual level and progressing to details (funnel) and then continuing with building on the details until the training ends in exploring even broader concepts than at the beginning.

Both the upright or inverted funnels represent two distinct cognitive patterns. A deductive learning or reasoning process (upright funnel) begins with general concepts and ends with specific outcomes. An inductive learning or reasoning process (inverted funnel) begins with specific circumstances and ends with general conclusions. Both achieve desired results depending on the nature of the material.

For example, sequencing topics for product knowledge training using the upright funnel design (deductive learning) might first present material about the product's origin, its initial design and manufacturing specifications, improvements over the years, and expanding applications, progressing to more specific information about the product's qualities, strengths, features, and so forth.

Sequencing topics for product knowledge training using the inverted funnel design would be the opposite (inductive learning) approach, following a topic sequence that starts with very specific information about the products features, qualities and benefits, and then progresses to broader information that speaks to the genesis and origins of the product's design and manufacturing.

Conceptually, both the deductive and inductive topic sequencing approaches give the trainer ways to organize a presentation with many topics. The result is a logical information flow that is generally pleasing to the adult learner.

DETERMINING A TRAINING MEDIUM

Training mediums are the vehicles by which training is delivered. Although instructor-led training is still by far the most popular method, its popularity dipped to 62 percent of all training in 2006, according to the Industry Report in *Training*, as compared to 70 percent the previous year. Other mediums showed increasing popularity, as 15 percent of training was delivered via e-learning, 14 percent via the virtual classroom, and 9 percent by other methods. The ASTD *2007 State of the Industry Report* indicated that 71.36 percent of all training hours were delivered by a live instructor in 2006, down from 74.70 percent in 2004. Technology-based training accounted for 30.28 percent of training hours in 2006, up from 11.47 percent five years earlier. Clearly, the number of instructor-led classroom training hours is declining, while the number of e-learning and/or the virtual classroom training hours is increasing.

Clearly, the dip in instructor-led classroom training in 2006 corresponds to an increase in using technology-assisted learning mediums. Virtual classroom training delivery, where the program is delivered via a trainer from another location, rose in popularity. Whereas only 6 percent of all training was delivered this way in 2000, its popularity rose to 14 percent in 2006, according to the *Training* Industry Report.

It appears that decisions regarding training mediums are most often influenced by the organization's size, its industry sector, and the training topic. According to the 2006 *Training* Industry Report, the favored training medium depended on the size of the organization. Small (fewer than one thousand employees) organizations delivered 62 percent of their training via an instructor-led classroom medium, compared to only 57 percent for large organizations of ten thousand or more employees. Conversely, large employers delivered 36 percent of their training via the online or virtual classroom route, as compared to only 29 percent for small organizations. This continues a trend that was observed in previous years.

Industry sectors seem to prefer particular ways to deliver training. The manufacturing sector clearly prefers classroom training; 84 percent of all training in this sector was delivered this way in 2006, up from 78 percent in 2005. This sector used self-study and virtual classroom training only 12 percent of the time. On the opposite end of the spectrum were technology, financial, and insurance sectors. They only delivered classroom training an average of 55 percent of the time, as opposed to using e-learning and virtual classroom training, an average of 40 percent of the time.

Certain topics seem to lend themselves to different training modalities. According to the 2006 Industry Report in *Training*, mandatory and compliance-related training topics (those required by government statute, licensing, and/or regulatory agency) were most amenable to online methods: 35 percent of these training topics were conducted either totally or mostly online. On the other hand, customer service, sales, and interpersonal skills training are predominantly in an instructor-led classroom medium with 55 percent of these topics using no online method.

Large organizations will probably continue to be the most frequent users of online and virtual classroom training mediums because they have strategically invested in the technology. Large organizations, especially in the technology, financial, and insurance sectors, must deal with significant and mandatory regulatory and compliance issues, and online/self-study training delivery seems to be best suited to these types of programs.

Conversely, small and medium-sized companies will probably continue to rely on instructor-led classroom training. They do not have the luxury of investing large amounts of capital in online or virtual classroom infrastructure, especially when it appears that the current classroom option already works for them. Most training programs that use technology-assisted training often blend it with instructor-led classroom training, according to the 2006 *Training* Industry Report. Small and medium-sized companies recognize that blending instructor-led classroom instruction with technology-assisted training would be nice, but is not a requirement to make the classroom training successful.

The most frequently offered training topics generally lend themselves to an instructor-led delivery medium. Organizations with priorities to train sales and customer service employees or executives, as well as conduct interpersonal skills training, still view instructor-led classroom training as the best way to change knowledge, skills, attitudes, and behavior.

Interaction with a human leader and other people in a classroom environment enhances the learning experience for these and other topics in ways that cannot be duplicated in purely an online or virtual classroom setting. Instructor-led classroom training blended with technology seems to be a trend that will continue to grow in popularity. Producing change is the bottom-line goal, and whatever training medium accomplishes change most effectively and efficiently will win the prize as the preferred training medium.

PROGRAM REQUIREMENTS AND CONSTRAINTS

The trainer needs to be sensitive to certain "must do–can't do" variables and account for them in the training program's design and delivery. Accommodating these factors gains organizational support for the training effort and allows training participants to focus fully on the training and not be distracted by external factors. The organization's unique history, culture experiences, and expectations will determine most of these training requirements and constraints. The trainer can create a design specifications document for each training event that includes the necessary specific requirements and restraints, along with recommendations to address them.

Length of Training Session. For training conducted on-site, organizations will typically devote a consistent time block for a training program. A morning (8:00 A.M. to noon), an afternoon (1:00 P.M. to 5:00 P.M.), or a lunch hour may be scheduled. This structure allows employees to take care of other business during the day.

Day of Week. Except for new employee orientation (which normally occurs on Mondays), training generally occurs on Tuesdays, Wednesdays, or Thursdays. Mondays and Fridays are avoided so that employees can take care of matters that accumulated from the past weekend, or clear items prior to the upcoming weekend.

Time of Year. Organizations are always busy, but there may be some periods during the year that are traditionally busier than others. The trainer should be sensitive to this dynamic and try to not schedule training during times when the entire organization is dealing with other priorities.

Location. Conducting programs on-site or off-site are decisions usually pre-determined by facilities and budgetary factors. There are strengths and weaknesses to either on-site or off-site delivery, and trainers must weigh these dynamics carefully before making this important decision.

Internal or External Trainer. If the medium is instructor-led classroom training, organizations usually have preferences for selecting a trainer who is either internal or external to the organization. Training topic, the availability of internal training talent with subject-matter expertise, previous experience, and budgetary considerations all influence the decision. Additional criteria will be reviewed in more detail in the next chapter on training delivery.

Classroom Learning Methods. Some organizations have definite preferences (and dislikes) for certain classroom learning methods. Role plays, small group discussions, instruments, videos, and audio-visuals are some of the methods that organizations have historically embraced or rejected. It is important for the trainer to ascertain this important information prior to the training.

Take-Away Materials. Organizations often have expectations related to the resource materials that will be distributed at training and retained by the trainees. The trainer should determine in advance the materials (if any) that trainees should take away with them from the training such as handout packets, workbooks, brochures, and/or binders.

Budgeting. Budgets are planning documents. Organizations create budgets as guides to, as best possible, plan for all income and expense items for a fiscal year. Training budgets represent a requirement and constraint that have to be adhered to.

Training does not usually generate income in the traditional sense. Knowledge, skill, attitude and behavior change are hopefully providing a quantifiable dollar impact. Return on the training investment will be fully discussed in Chapter 8. This section on budgeting will focus on training expenses.

ALLOCATING RESOURCES

Organizations must decide how much money they can afford to spend on training. There are several ways to calculate the appropriate budget allocation for training. A popular method is to target training expenditures as a percentage of annual payroll (without benefits and taxes).

ASTD's *2007 State of the Industry Report* found that 2.33 percent of total annual payroll dollars were spent on training, a flat number since 2003. The March 2007 issue of *Training* reported its list of 125 companies with the top-ranked employee-sponsored workforce training and development programs. Training budgets as a percentage of annual payroll were reported by sixty-nine of the 125 companies. On average, 4.8 percent of annual payroll was the spent on training in these sixty-nine companies.

ALLOCATING EXPENSES

The greatest percentage of training's budget is usually devoted to training employee salaries. However, even with the increase in the number of training staff and dollars budgeted for training in 2006, total dollars allocated to training salaries actually declined from 2005. This is a continuing trend; in 1998, training staff salaries were 69 percent of total training expenditures. In 1992, training salaries were 71 percent of total training expenditures. The percent of training expenditures devoted to training salaries was 65 percent in 2006, its lowest level over the previous five years.

This phenomenon occurred because of the changing mix of jobs within training departments. Past reliance on higher-priced trainers and instructors has been replaced by greater numbers of lower-salaried content developers and technology specialists in response to the rise in technology-based training. Rather than employing a team of trainers, more companies are willing to outsource training delivery (to be discussed more thoroughly in Chapter 6). Although a higher-priced option in the near term (external consultants or providers of training earned an average of $103,649 annually, according to *Training* magazine's 2006 salary survey, compared to an average classroom instructor or trainer annual salary of $60,213), outsourcing represents a hedge just in case the economy goes bad and companies need to cut full-time employees.

This trend is likely to continue. Senior staff trainers (many of the baby-boomer generation) will continue to age and retire, freeing up training dollars for younger, lower-salaried and less experienced trainers as well as financial resources to support e-learning. Questions about the sustaining health of the economy will continue to arise, causing organizations to continue to rely on a flexible staffing mix of employees and consultants.

With 65 percent of the training budget currently devoted to training staff salaries (including professional trainers and administrative support staff), the remaining 35 percent of the training budget are allocated to the following line items:

1. *Seminars and Conferences:* Training by outside providers or contractors, either at the organization's location or off-site, not including trainee travel and per diem expenses.
2. *Custom Materials:* Materials tailored or designed by outside vendors specifically for the organization for instructor-led classroom training, computer courseware, or online programs.
3. *Off-the-Shelf Materials:* Prepackaged materials purchased from outside vendors such as computer courseware, books, videos, CD-ROM/DVDs.

4. *Technology-Based Training:* Any training involving technology for delivery it, such as web-based training, computerized self-study (including CD-ROMs, DVDs, or diskette) satellite or broadcast TV, and video, audio, or teleconferencing.
5. *Traditional Training Materials:* Any training materials not involving technology for delivery, such as textbooks, workbooks, games, and self-assessment/group learning instruments.
6. *Other Expenditures:* Trainee travel and per diem costs, training classroom furnishings, training class refreshments, copying, and office supplies.

The overall allocation of training budget expenditures to non-salary line items will depend most heavily on the training mediums used by the organization. Additionally, budgets should be created for individual training programs in order to more accurately track return on investment figures for each program. Each program expenditure would vary depending on the medium mix and level of consultant, vendor, material, and technology support.

Management's Role. The organization's management team significantly influences—some would say determines—the organization's environment and culture. Perceived management support is a significant factor in training's success; perceived lack of management support is a significant factor in training's failure to produce necessary change. Acquiring knowledge, learning new skills, and exhibiting new attitudes and behaviors requires training, but training alone is not sufficient. Public endorsement and support by management is essential. Management's role in the training program must be accounted for in the training plan. It can take on many different levels and types of involvement.

The management team can provide a range of participation that, at minimum, starts with the management team guaranteeing that the employees they supervise will have the opportunity to attend training. This may seem like an obvious point, but attending training requires time away from daily job duties. Management must commit to training as a priority and should not deny employee access. The management team must agree that preempting training is unacceptable; it undermines the training effort by sending a message that training is unimportant. This rule should apply whether training is on-site or off-site. Change is made more difficult if people cannot participate fully in the change effort. Two examples on either end of the continuum clearly demonstrate this phenomenon.

A large aerospace organization in Southern California contracted with a recognized consultant in project management to conduct a one-day on-site seminar for twelve department managers. The cost of the program was $12,000 and the organization determined that spending $1,000 per manager on this important topic was a good investment. The training needs assessment had determined that frequently missed project deadlines and other issues related to timely project completion were a significant barrier to enterprise-wide strategic goal accomplishment. The need for a change in the manager's knowledge, skills, attitudes, and behaviors related to project management were paramount. Notification of the training date was sent well in advance to all managers, including their senior director, and schedules were arranged and cleared accordingly so all twelve managers would be in town and prepared to attend the program.

On the day before the training program, the senior director decided that due to slipping deadlines and multiple project management issues, he would only send three managers to the training. Three managers attended and the organization spent $12,000 to train three managers instead of twelve. As the result of the senior manager's actions; cost per trainee skyrocketed, the untrained managers' behavior will continue to be a barrier to goal accomplishment, and the message was sent that training was not a priority. The perception is that the next training program that is arranged will potentially have a similar outcome.

In a major market cellular provider, the general manager had a rule that if managers or supervisors wanted to schedule employees out of a training session, they had to receive advance permission directly from him. The message was clear: Training was a high priority. There had better be an extraordinary reason to schedule someone out. With this rule in place, in the two years when that general manager was in charge of that major cellular market, managers and supervisors never once requested an exception to remove an employee from a training program.

The message the senior manager team sends regarding the importance of training cannot be overestimated. The range of management team participation grows from there. If the training is in-house, management may support the training effort by assisting with training program design, providing introductory remarks before training sessions, identifying and/or bringing in experts from the field, facilitating vendor support and involvement, assisting with internal marketing, or conducting classroom presentations and evaluations. Some managers may be more willing and/or able to assist than others; that is fine as long as each commits to making sure that all of their direct reports will attend.

Summary

1. Review the main precepts of adult learning theory as conceived by Malcolm Knowles.

2. Incorporate adult learning concepts into the training program design.

3. Create a program design plan that clearly outlines specific requirements and constraints unique to the organization and the specific training program.

4. Design training goals that clearly state expected training outcomes.

5. Construct and adhere to a training budget.

6. Clarify management's role in supporting training.

CHAPTER FIVE

TRAINING DELIVERY

"Try to realize it's all within yourself, no one else can make you change."
GEORGE HARRISON

PURPOSE

This chapter will enable you to accomplish the following:

- Review instructor competencies and how they impact the training experience
- Identify organizational parameters to help determine training delivery methods
- Describe the unique characteristics of ten instructional methods
- Identify effective instructor behaviors and techniques
- Examine using technology to assist training delivery

OVERVIEW

Research studies have uncovered key competencies and behaviors that facilitate a positive training experience. It is crucial for the training professional to ensure that trainers possess and demonstrate these traits. An examination of significant organizational factors will determine the most effective and efficient training delivery methods. For instructor-led classroom training, ten different instructional methods will be described. The strengths and weaknesses of other training delivery methods are reviewed including technology-assisted training.

Achieving Training Goals

Once goals are identified through a training design process, the training professional must evaluate the best ways to deliver training in order to achieve desired training results. A number of critical factors must be assessed before decisions can be made to determine the most effective ways to deliver training.

Assessments must be made to determine whether the appropriate instructor competencies are housed within the organization. Take into account organizational culture, budget, training topic(s), time availability, technology availability, urgency, and target audience location, all critical factors when making training delivery decisions. Trainers must decide how to package and present appropriate materials and determine the most effective classroom techniques to create a training experience that will change knowledge, skills, attitudes, and behaviors. Consider technology assisted delivery as well.

Instructor Competencies: Applicable Research

The classroom trainer's mission is to achieve the training program's goals, achieved when trainees demonstrate changes in knowledge, skills, attitudes, and behaviors. Instructor competence is critical to facilitating change in the classroom.

When trainees are asked about training programs they have attended and the trainer characteristics that left either a positive or negative impression, their answers are consistent. Positive trainer attributes include lively and enthusiastic, knowledgeable about the subject, and a pleasant and easy-to-understand speaking voice. Negative trainer attributes include dull, boring, not interested or knowledgeable in the subject, and monotonous voice.

Some trainer attributes receive mixed reviews from trainees. Humorous, organized, good-looking and well-dressed often fall into this category—important and influential for some trainees, not important to others. Trainees who experience a trainer with positive attributes will be more likely to embrace the training experience. Trainees who experience a trainer with negative attributes will be less likely to embrace the training experience. Trainees in denial and/or resistance mode, as related to their willingness and/or ability to change, will seize on a trainer's negative attributes as another reason to maintain the status quo.

Much research has been devoted to the study of evaluating trainer behavior and associated effectiveness. Two studies are especially important.

International Competency Study

The International Board of Standards for Training, Performance and Instruction (IBSTPI) issued the results of its Instructor Competencies Study (2003) and found five main competency categories;

1. Professional Foundations

- Communicates effectively
- Updates and improves one's professional knowledge and skills
- Complies with established ethical and legal standards
- Establishes and maintains professional credibility

2. Planning and Preparation

- Plans instructional methods and materials
- Prepares for instruction

3. Instructional Methods and Strategies

- Stimulates and sustains learner motivation and engagement
- Demonstrates effective presentation skills
- Demonstrates effective facilitation skills
- Demonstrates effective questioning skills
- Provides clarification and feedback
- Promotes retention of knowledge and skills
- Promotes transfer of knowledge and skills

4. Assessment and Evaluation

- Assesses learning and performance
- Evaluates instructional effectiveness

5. Management

- Manages an environment that fosters learning and performance
- Manages the instructional process through appropriate use of technology

CALDWELL AND MARCEL

Caldwell and Marcel (1985) studied and ranked the effectiveness of two types of variables that instructors display.

Presage Variables. Presage variables are characteristics that the trainer brings to the classroom situation and thus influence the learning process. The most important presage variables, listed in order of importance, are

- Knowledge of subject matter
- Good speaking ability
- Enthusiastic, positive attitude
- Well-prepared, good organization
- Depth of understanding
- Patience
- Poise, confidence

Trainees will be more likely to acquire knowledge, skills, attitudes, and behaviors if they feel the trainer is knowledgeable in the subject. The trainer who has good speaking ability and is able to communicate knowledge in a pleasing manner (e.g., good voice quality or projection, enunciation, and modulation) will be more likely to achieve the desired training goals. If the trainer has strong subject knowledge and good speaking ability, but is not enthusiastic about the subject, the ability to achieve training goals will be reduced. Trainers who are knowledgeable and possess great speaking ability may make the mistake at the beginning of a training session by verbally and/or non-verbally communicating, "I know this is a boring subject, but let's make the best use of the time we have together." If the trainer says it's a boring subject, the trainees will not be fully engaged in the learning/change process.

These first three variables—knowledge of the subject, good speaking ability, and enthusiasm—are critical for the trainer to achieve program goals. The remaining four variables—well-prepared, depth of understanding, patience, and confidence—are also important if training goals are to be achieved.

Process Variables. Process variables are the behaviors that influence the learning process through the sorts of relationships/ interactions the trainer develops with the group of trainees. Process variables are also critically important to training program success.

The most important process variables, listed in order of importance, are

- Retains control of class—keeps focus on the agenda, achieves observable results and keeps students on task and topic
- Gives feedback and positive reinforcement
- Behaves fairly and impartially
- Communicates at the students level, using language and examples appropriate to the level of the class
- Involves students in the lesson through questions, problem solving, simulations, etc.
- Shows interest in each learner
- Listens attentively and responsively
- Communicates clear objectives

Control of the class does not suggest an autocratic, heavy-handed approach that squelches interaction and individual expression. Control in this context means maintained focus on an agenda that is designed to achieve desired outcomes. A trainer who loses control of the class, and thus the ability to move the trainees through an agenda to a training goal, stands little chance of facilitating change in knowledge, skills, attitudes, or behavior, even if he or she follows all of the other presage and process variables.

The remaining process variables determine the quality of the classroom learning environment. Providing feedback, positive reinforcement, fairness, impartiality, and active listening are all trainer behaviors that facilitate trainee support, openness, and safety while they explore new knowledge.

Effective classroom trainers must be knowledgeable, enthusiastic, and possess good speaking ability. They must also demonstrate effective interpersonal communication and relationship-building skills with trainees. Familiarity and command of the key presage and process variables are vital to trainer performance and training program success.

USING INTERNAL AND EXTERNAL RESOURCES

Designing and delivering a training experience that changes participant knowledge, skills, attitudes, and behaviors is a challenging undertaking. The training professional needs to determine whether the competencies to achieve this task are housed within the organization and if they are available for training purposes. If they aren't, the vendor community is ready, willing, and able to deliver.

The beauty of a training program custom-designed and delivered by internal personnel is their intimate familiarity with the organization. The program will be tailored to meet the training professional's requirements and the target audience's specific needs. Unique industry, organization, job- and situation-specific training program content and delivery facilitates achieving the trainer's specific learning goals. Needs assessment findings unique to the organization can also be incorporated into the training materials. These programs are especially effective and cost efficient when needing to be repeated many times because of the nature of the material and the target audience.

For example, a San Diego theme park requires that all employees follow a new employee orientation (NEO) process that is similar for many organizations. Every new employee must complete a two-day NEO training program before being allowed to work in any department. It is an internally custom-designed and delivered instructor-led classroom experience presented by a combination of theme park trainers, human resource professionals, and departmental employees in a subject-matter expert role. A combination of off-the-shelf and custom-made instructional videos are used to augment their presentations on subjects, including mission and vision, safety, theft prevention, and customer service. Department personnel conduct first day hands-on, on-the-job training with new employees once they are assigned to a work station. On day two, employees perform their job tasks alongside peer employees with the ability to initiate direct phone contact with a supervisor if questions and/or problems arise. It is the theme park's goal to instill desired knowledge, skills, attitudes, and behaviors with employees at the earliest possible time.

But customized program design is resource-intensive and time-consuming; if cost-efficiency, training project overload and/or competency gaps are issues and urgency is a requirement, the training professional may decide to use internal resources to deliver training but look to an external resource for program design.

Training magazine's 2006 Industry Report found that 30 percent of the organizations surveyed used external resources to design training despite the significant additional expense. Customized training products are designed specifically for the organization purchasing the product and for the target audience it intends to train. Customized products produced by external resources generally possess the same strengths and weaknesses as off-the-shelf packages that will be discussed in the next chapter.

Conversely, the training professional may determine that in-house expertise is available to design the training program, but the organization lacks the ability to deliver it. In this case, outsourcing instruction is indicated. According to *Training's* 2006 Industry Report, approximately 44 percent of the organizations surveyed stated that they used external trainers to deliver some of their training.

The training professional may determine that some training design and/or delivery expertise must be brought in from outside to meet the organization's training needs. Outsourcing will be fully discussed in the next chapter.

OFF-THE-SHELF DESIGN AND DELIVERY

Off-the-shelf training products (off-the-web might be a more appropriate descriptor), refers to packaged training products on particular topic(s) that the organization purchases and delivers to trainees as is. Such packages often include a DVD, workbook, assorted group training activities with instructions for administration, and lecture or facilitation notes. Like any training-provider option, this approach has its strengths and weaknesses.

Strengths

Off-the-shelf products are usually strong in their design and consistent message delivery. The materials have already been created, so there is no delay in delivering training to the target audience. The information is usually well-researched and produced, easy for the trainer to deliver, and pleasing to the trainees. The trainer can deliver a consistent message session after session because the training package includes the scheduled agenda of lectures, interactive learning activities, and videos. This is an important advantage if large numbers of people must be trained on the same topic in multiple locations. The training professional wants each group of trainees to receive a consistent, positive training experience, hear the same message, and ultimately to experience equivalent, desired changes. Using the same physical materials at every session ensures consistency.

An evaluation process is usually built into the product in the form of tests that trainees must complete satisfactorily at the end of each module to proceed to the next. This process ensures and documents information retention.

Weaknesses

Off-the-shelf training packages must be purchased as is. They are meant for a generic, mass audience and are not designed or tailored to meet organizational or industry-specific learning needs. This lack of precision may inhibit change in knowledge, skills, attitudes, and behavior in the specific target audience.

Off-the-shelf training packages, if led by live instructors, require skilled facilitators to lead trainees through the training experience. The vendor can provide these facilitators (at significant expense), or the organization's training professional, with preparation by the vendor, can facilitate the training. Depending on the scope of the effort, additional individuals in the organization may need to be identified and trained as facilitators along with the training professional. These investments in time, effort, and personnel must be factored into the training budget to determine if using such a product is the most effective and efficient way to proceed.

Although some vendors provide updates to packaged programs for an additional cost, the training professional must recognize that such packages, like groceries, have a shelf life. They are valid and relevant for a finite period of time before industry and other trends change, and the materials become obsolete. Unlike groceries, off-the-shelf products do not have an expiration date on the package, so estimating shelf life is difficult. For this kind of program to be cost-effective for long-term budgeting purposes, the training professional needs to project the anticipated number of trainees who will use the product before it is anticipated to become obsolete to determine whether it is a cost-effective investment.

Training Delivery Via Live Instructor or Technology (or Both)

Most training is delivered by a live instructor—62 percent of all programs according to the 2006 Industry Report, 65 percent of all training hours according to the ASTD *2007 State of the Industry Report*. Self-study e-learning is on the rise and accounts for 15 percent; the virtual classroom format is used in training delivery 14 percent of the time. When technology-assisted delivery is used, it is often in conjunction with a live trainer to form a blended learning format. As the 2006 *Training* Industry Report suggests, factors such as budget, industry-type, training topic, and the target audience's location influence the training professional's decision to use technology in training delivery.

Larger organizations (ten thousand or more employees) generally have the budget needed to procure and maintain training-related hardware and software that smaller organizations cannot afford. They must also be able to train large numbers of employees in relatively short time periods; technology-assisted methodology can be the most effective and efficient delivery system for them. One of the leading financial services companies in the United States, trains its employees using a blended approach of instructor-led classroom delivery supported by technology.

Technology and financial services organizations tend to use technology in training more than manufacturing, retail, and healthcare institutions according to *Training's* 2006 Industry Report. For example, a San Diego-based telecommunications organization trains its employees with an entirely web-based program.

Employees are provided a series of learning modules on topics related to company products, services, and processes that they are expected to complete within a prescribed time period. Completed questionnaires at the conclusion of each module serve as documentation of successful completion.

According to *Training's* 2006 Industry Report, mandatory/compliance training and information technology and systems training are most often delivered using technology, while interpersonal skills, customer service, and sales training are most often delivered by live instructors. Blended learning approaches seem to be gaining popularity in both camps. Live instructors are used more often to supplement pure training delivery, and technology is used to augment the instructor-led classroom training experience.

When the majority of trainees are located on-site, the training professional can reach them through either instructor-led or on-site, technology-assisted delivery. If the majority of trainees are off-site but in one location, they can be reached the same way if provisions can be made to transport the instructor and/or technology to that site.

When the majority of trainees are off-site but in different locations, the logistics of bringing them together for training is probably prohibitive. Delivering training under this circumstance will likely be achieved through a technology-assisted approach.

Using Subject-Matter Experts

Subject-matter experts (SMEs) are often technically oriented and skilled employees whose expertise makes them invaluable contributors to training program design and training. Organizations generally prefer attempting to turn SMEs into trainers, as opposed to trying to turn trainers into SMEs. To be effective trainers, SMEs must be proficient at performing the technical skills themselves, transferring their expertise to learners, dealing with learner feelings in a constructive and confidence-building way, and handling learners whose expertise ranges from beginner to advanced. So although subject-matter experts must be knowledgeable in the subject matter, they must also possess appropriate instructor competencies to deliver training effectively.

Organizations like using SMEs as trainers because they have a thorough understanding of the subject, they relate well to the learners' technical training needs, and as fellow employees, they generally have instant credibility in the eyes of the trainees. Hospitals routinely use designated in-house staff to conduct regular in-service training with employees on knowledge and skills care-related equipment, processes, procedures, and techniques.

Concurrently, organizations have some concerns about using SMEs as trainers, due to their lack of training competency. Their effectiveness is diminished if they are not well-versed in adult learning theory. Because SMEs know much more information about the subject than they need to convey in training, they have difficulty setting priorities, deciding what content to include and what to exclude. Consequently, they may overload learners with information unrelated to job needs and training goals.

For SMEs to be used effectively to deliver training, they must be viewed as adult educators—like all trainers. They must have knowledge of the subject, and they must possess effective classroom skills in order for their training to achieve desired changes in the participants' knowledge, skills, attitudes, and behavior.

SMEs who are not trainers must be trained in classroom techniques in order to effectively conduct training. Training SMEs to deliver training can be performed by either in-house trainers or external training providers depending on organizational preference.

TRAIN-THE-TRAINER

Training SMEs and/or other employees to train others is another method used to deliver training to the organization's target audience(s). As with all training delivery methods, there are strengths and weaknesses to this approach.

Strengths

It is more efficient and less expensive for on-site employees to provide training programs in multiple or outlying locations than to transport employees from outlying areas to one central location for training. The train-the-trainer model minimizes wear and tear on internal training staff that are relieved of the responsibility to conduct multiple sessions at several outlying locations.

The trainers selected for this assignment need to demonstrate requisite trainer competencies such as knowledge of the topic, good speaking ability, enthusiasm, and interpersonal and facilitative skills. Employees possessing these skill sets are naturals for the role and are most likely to be successful. Tangentially, this training model represents a career-development opportunity for the employees selected as trainers since presentation and facilitation skills are transferable to a wide variety of jobs.

Trainees will generally be more trusting of, and empathetic toward, a fellow employee in the role of trainer than an external trainer. They will be more likely to support the training effort and the implicit desire for change.

Weaknesses

It is a stretch to ask newly trained trainers to effectively navigate potentially treacherous waters to successfully conducting a training program. These are employees who were hired to do something else being asked to take on additional, different, and very challenging responsibilities that take time and experience to master.

Training trainers is a training effort of its own for the training professional. Preparing trainers for the daunting task of leading training programs requires a combination of imparting knowledge about the subject (if not an SME) and group leadership and facilitation skills. Employees selected from the ranks are generally better at one or the other; those skilled at both are rare. Designing and conducting train-the-trainer sessions is an arduous and time-consuming process for the training professional who must foresee that investing in this effort will pay off in the long term. Hiring an external trainer to conduct train-the-trainer training is an expense that must be incorporated into the budget.

While most trainees will support their fellow employees leading a training program, some employee trainers may be reluctant to take on the role of training leader with peers, and some peers may be uncomfortable being led by someone they consider an equal who they feel is not qualified to train others. While many will see selection for the trainer role as a long-term career-development opportunity, the organizational message may be "We want you to do this trainer role, but we still expect you to meet your current job expectations." The perceived long-term career payoff may not be sufficient to overcome the short-term pain of substantially increased job responsibilities.

Newly trained trainers will, by their nature, deliver training programs differently from one another. Even the same trainer doing multiple sessions of the same topic with the same agenda will rarely have one training program go exactly the same as another one. There is a natural amount of variability that comes with different trainers and trainees. Natural variability, even following the same training agenda, will produce outcomes that vary.

Informal OJT

Employees in need of guidance will find it anywhere they can. Organizations without a formal, structured training program leave the learning process to chance. Employees will find mentor(s) to shadow, absorbing their knowledge and emulating their attitudes and behaviors. Hopefully, the model they follow is positive; if not, misinformation will spread, unmet performance expectations will occur, and a significant barrier to the organization's ability to achieve its goals and follow its mission will have been created.

Classroom Techniques

Delivering successful instructor-led classroom training is both art and science. Successful training, training that achieves its goals, requires a balanced blend of method and imagination. Too much method and too little imagination could leave participants bored, stifled, and uninterested in changing. Too little method and too much imagination could leave participants dazed, confused, and wondering what change they are supposed to embrace (and why).

There are no right and wrong ways to design and deliver classroom training. There are instruction methods that, with practice and repetition, seem to be more successful than others.

There are no guarantees that, for instance, if
A, then B, then C, and so on, that the trair
achieve desired results. The best strategy is for
and demonstrate their instructor competency
instructional methods and effective classroom ski
chances for a successful training outcome.

INSTRUCTIONAL METHODS

Classroom instructors package training content into a series of
instructional methods that are delivered to participants. Material
is covered through lectures, role plays, small group discussion,
instruments, and other methods. Care and attention must also be
given to the order in which the trainer presents these activities.

Instructional methods determine the interaction level between
instructor and trainees which sets the tone for the classroom environment. Two-way communication is essential for knowledge,
skills, attitudes, and behavior change to occur.

INSTRUCTOR CONTROL AND LEARNER FREEDOM

The range of instructional options the trainer can select is influenced by the relative balance of two variables—instructor control
and learner freedom. These factors have an inverse relationship -
the higher the level of instructor control, the lower the level of
learner freedom and vise versa.

They form a dynamic tension that determines the classroom
learning environment and the interaction level between instructor and trainee. Their appropriate use and placement order in
the training program can create optimal learning conditions and
have a profound effect on the behavior of training program participants. Using either type of instructional method to excess will
be detrimental to their training experience. Too much instructor control creates the dynamic of one-way communication from
instructor to trainee. Too little instructor control creates a cha-
otic dynamic that prevents the agenda from being followed and
the training program goals from being accomplished. The trainer
may use any or all of the following instruction methods.

Instructor Reading

Reading to the group provides the highest level of instructor control and the lowest level of learner freedom. Reading literally means the instructor reads information to the group. This technique is appropriate for very short periods of time to impart a specific passage of information. Used with frequency and for any extended period of time, it can be stifling and boring. Undergraduate and graduate students, as well as trainees, may have experienced hearing famous instructors read long passages from their books to their class throughout their lectures. Brilliant professors, authors, consultants, and trainers may write interesting books, but trainees who are read to for long periods of time aren't likely to acquire or enhance their knowledge. If instructor control is too high for too long (thus learner freedom is too low for too long), desired changes are less likely. How long is too long is a judgment the trainer makes sensing the audience. Instructor A reading long passages from his or her book on performance evaluations is not going to change the knowledge, skill, attitudes, or behavior of the managers in the audience in conducting performance evaluations.

Instructor Lecture

Lecture is one step down the escalator from reading in terms of less instructor control and one step higher in terms of learner freedom—but not by much. Lecture maintains a high degree of instructor control as well as a low level of learner freedom. It is an instructional method that, used in excess, causes learners to lose interest in the presented information and compromises accomplishing training goals. Interaction between instructor and trainee is limited when most of the communication is one-way. And, if the instructor doesn't allow questions from the trainees, there is no opportunity for trainees to learn from each other. Instructor A conducting long lectures about performance evaluations as the predominant instruction method will not change trainee behavior.

Experiential Lecture

The experiential lecture is somewhat lower in terms of instructor control because the instructor not only presents material in a lecture format but also requests the trainees to interject their own perceptions and experiences related to the subject. The instructor is not doing all the instructing/controlling but is including the trainees in the instruction. The level of instructor control is lower and, conversely, the level of learner freedom is higher. The learners not only learn from the instructor, but they are also receiving information from the other people in the room. There is a better communication balance between instructor and trainee, and trainees have the opportunity to learn from each other. For example, the instructor encouraging the manager audience to share their successes and failures conducting performance evaluations is a learning activity that may have a significant impact on the knowledge, skill, attitudes, and behavior of the trainees.

Small Group Discussion

Small group discussion is next on the classroom techniques continuum. In this instructional method, instructor control is limited to giving the small group (minimum three trainees) a topic to discuss and/or a task to complete and report back to the large group at a specified time. The trainees have the freedom to proceed and discuss the topic as they wish without instructor involvement. Interaction between instructor and trainees is enhanced as trainees report their findings to the large group. Interaction between trainees is also greater than in previously discussed classroom techniques. An example of an effective small group discussion activity asks trainees to share their single most important tip about conducting performance evaluations in their group and have each small group report their tip list to the large group.

Participant Training

Participant training is an instructional method in which a trainee, either by design or happenstance, takes on the role of trainer to demonstrate a specific technique and/or behavior. Its placement as a lower instructor control/higher learner freedom type of activity is self-evident. An example is a safety training session during which someone in the audience shows the rest of the trainees how to operate a particular piece of equipment in a desirable, safe way. In hospital safety training, for instance, a trainee might demonstrate how to safely lift a particularly heavy patient. Adults learning from peers can be a very powerful and positive force toward the ultimate goal of changing trainee behavior. If a training participant has expertise to perform a task that is equal to that of the instructor, then it is valuable to ask this person to lead a segment of the learning activity for the rest of the group. Having a trainee demonstrate his or her successful technique for telling a direct report, in a performance evaluation setting, that the job performance in a key result area has not met expectations will be very instructive and influential with the other trainers.

Case Study

The case study offers an even greater opportunity for learner freedom with less instructor control. The trainer presents a case or scenario that depicts a situation related to the training topic to which trainees apply problem-solving and decision-making skills. Trainees, either individually or in small groups, analyze the case and make recommendations to address the issue. Executive management programs and university curricula, most notably the Harvard Business School, base their course of study on presenting a series of case studies of actual business situations for students to analyze.

A subset of this instructional method in action is the in-box (or in-basket) exercise. Trainees are given a set of memos, letters, e-mails, an organizational chart, a calendar of scheduled meetings, and other items that might hypothetically be in a manager's in-box upon arriving at a new or existing job. Individually, the trainee must respond to each item within a given time frame (usually one hour) by either (1) delaying a decision about the issue; (2) referring the issue to someone else in the organization; or (3) making a decision about the issue. After the trainees have completed writing how they would respond to each memo and e-mail, the trainer processes the exercise in a large group experiential lecture that reviews the various possible actions that could have been taken with each in-box item and the ramifications of the trainee's decision-making process on time management, delegating, leadership style, problem solving and decision making. The feedback to the trainee is invaluable.

Consider the value of a case study that asks each trainee to complete a sample performance evaluation form when provided data describing Employee A's job performance in several key result areas. Such practice in writing evaluative narrative statements will most likely improve the trainee's knowledge, skills, attitudes, and behavior when performing this very challenging task prior to a real performance evaluation session.

Role Play

Role play is a simulation exercise in which one or more people is asked to behave in a particular way so the other person or people in the role play have an opportunity to practice how to deal with such an individual. This method is most appropriate to help trainees deal with problems and decisions related to human interactions and relationships. The level of learner freedom is higher than in the previously described instructional methods, and the instructor control is significantly lower—the trainer presents the guidelines and the role player(s) take it from there, bringing to the role their own personalities and behavioral tendencies. Often, the trainer will take on one of the roles in an initial run-through to model the behavior the trainees should emulate. The appropriate uses of this instructional method abound: training customer service employees how to deal with irate customers; training managers and supervisors how to conduct work performance counseling sessions; and training managers and supervisors how to conduct a face-to-face performance evaluation discussion. Not only do the participants learn from their role play, but the audience members also learn by watching the role play and wondering what they would do similarly or differently if they were in the situation.

Instrumentation

Instrumentation is the instructional method of choice when the desired result involves participants gaining further insight or feedback into their own styles of behavior. Usually, instruments are structured as a series of paper-and-pencil questions the participant scores at the end of a designated time period. Instruments have been created to give training participants feedback about themselves on everything from communication to conflict style, from preferred leadership styles to preferred problem-solving and decision-making styles. Instruments demonstrate a higher form of learner freedom and a lower level of instructor control than previously mentioned instructional methods. They are highly interactive activities that promote a great deal of two-way communication between trainer and trainees.

Although guided by instructions and interpretive feedback from the trainer, the learner makes many assumptions and draws many conclusions about the meaning of the data and how it relates to them. Instruments such as the Performance Appraisal Skills Inventory are designed to alert managers to their performance evaluation weak spots with tips for improvement. For example, one tip might include paying closer attention to the tasks assigned to different employees to address motivation issues.

Structured Experiences

The structured experience is an activity that puts participants through a specific experience, with both the trainer and trainees processing the outcomes as they relate to the training topic. A multitude of simple, yet powerful structured experiences are available to the training professional and can be found in vendor catalogs like HRDQ and from publishers such as Pfeiffer. As with instrumentation, there are structured experiences that relate to the full gamut of training topics. They promote a lot of interaction between trainer and trainees. Similarly, with guidance from the trainer, the learners have tremendous freedom to apply the insights and outcomes of the experience to their own knowledge, skill, attitudes, and behaviors.

A favorite structured experience in the performance evaluation realm is the activity called Evaluate Your Famous Employee. Trainees are given a list of famous people and asked to select one (with a job title) that they pretend has been their direct report for the past year. The trainees complete a sample performance evaluation form for that famous person, complete with ratings, evaluation narratives, and future goals.

Leaderless Group Activity (or T-Group)

The leaderless group activity is the ultimate on the instructor control/learner freedom continuum. It is also referred to as the T-Group because of its association with Tavistock, a town in England where Sigmund Freud founded the Tavistock Institute and pioneered work in behavioral science that was later brought to the United States by behaviorist and Institute director Kurt Lewin in 1933. The instructor exerts little control and formal leadership because the group (usually ten to twelve participants) and their activity is largely unstructured with a very flexible agenda.

The trainer gives the group an imaginary task to perform for a specific time period (twenty minutes, for example), such as deciding as a group where to go for lunch or how to spend an imaginary $1 million gift. The training leader gives no other guidance and lets the group go. It is usually helpful to have observers posted around the room with each taking notes on what a selected group of trainees (usually no more than three) do and say. This information is fed back to the participants at the conclusion of their discussion, when they receive information related to the roles and behavior(s) they exhibit in a group. A short experiential lecture follows that focuses on developing more awareness and understanding of group processes, including the task and relationship aspects of leadership and group behavior.

ORDER OF INSTRUCTIONAL METHODS

Ten instructional methods have been presented in sequential order to demonstrate the progressive and inverse relationship between the dynamics of instructor control and learner freedom. Each creates an interaction level between trainer and trainees to form a classroom environment that has a profound effect on learning - facilitating change in trainee knowledge, skills, attitudes, and behavior. One of the classroom trainer's challenges is to determine which instructional methods to use, their content, and the best order in which to present them. These decisions will create an optimal classroom learning environment, maximize interaction between trainer and trainees and between trainees, and provide the greatest opportunity to achieve goals.

It is generally preferable for the trainer to start a training program with an activity of high instructor control. A lecture format for communicating trainer introductions, program agenda, training program goals, and initial questions and answers is appropriate. Next, shift to an activity of lower instructor control and higher learner freedom, such as an instrument, a structured experience, or a small-group discussion. Following this activity, shifting to an instructional method of higher instructor control and lower learner freedom such as a lecture, is appropriate.

Experienced trainers anecdotally report the format that seems to work best uses an alternating back-and-forth pattern of high to low instructor control and learner freedom activities. This pattern of using instructional methods keeps training participants engaged, participating, and moving toward the goals of the training session.

TECHNOLOGY-ASSISTED DELIVERY

Training professionals must determine the best ways to address training needs that have been uncovered via a needs assessment. Instructor-led classroom training, although still the most commonly used delivery method, is increasingly augmented by technology. Previously discussed organizational requirements and constraints will help determine whether blending classroom training with technology-assisted delivery is the method that will provide the greatest opportunity to change trainee knowledge, skills, attitudes, and behaviors.

SELF-STUDY (SELF-PACED) AND/OR ONLINE TRAINING

Self-study (also known as self-paced) and/or online training, accessed via the web or software loaded onto a computer or server, represents a departure from the typical classroom model. Employees receive training via their individual computer terminals through delivery of topic-specific video and/or text. Participants progress through a series of subtopic modules and demonstrate successful completion through an interactive instrument such as a multiple-choice test.

Confidence seems to be growing in the ability of technology-assisted training to deliver results. According to the 2005 Industry Report, 70 percent of formal training was conducted in the classroom with live instructors, compared with 7 percent that was delivered via the online self-study method. The 2006 study showed a shift; 62 percent of formal training was conducted in the classroom with a live instructor, as compared to 15 percent online/self-study.

Strengths

The strength of this training approach is imbedded in its title; trainees can progress through self-paced courses at their own speed and convenience. Trainees regulate the presentation flow and subsequent information absorption with the goal to maximize learning. Content consistency is guaranteed, and the trainer knows that trainees have demonstrated some mastery of the material via a percent of correct scores on a completed end-of-module questionnaire.

Weaknesses

Some doubt that desired changes in knowledge, skills, and behavior can occur in isolation. A group classroom experience provides a powerful change dynamic that is not possible with solo learning. The classroom affords many positive training aspects, such as superior presenter skills, live and interesting classmate interaction, and powerful role-play simulation that facilitate learning but that are not available in a self-paced or online format. Others say the classroom affords experiences that are also detrimental to the training experience, such as inferior presentation skills, distracting classmate interaction, and ineffective role-play simulations that impede learning.

TELECONFERENCING

Teleconferencing as a training delivery system is an option in either a web-based or closed circuit delivery system. In either case, teleconference training is instructor-led from a remote location.

Strengths

Logistically, it is far more desirable to deliver the same training message to numerous remote locations at the same time, thus avoiding the expense and nightmare of herding employees to a central point for a series of mass meetings. Facilitators, like trained trainers, can be located at each site and prepared ahead of time to handle questions, answers, and follow-up items once the teleconference is completed. It's certainly a real-time training delivery system, as opposed to the dog-and-pony road show of the dedicated training professional(s) delivering a series of presentations to employees located at remote sites. Completing a multiple-location training cycle could take weeks, months, or years, depending on the number of trainers and the size of the organization.

Webinars, a seminar delivered via the web to individuals logged on to their computers, is a version of a teleconference. An instructor in a remote location leads the webinar.

Weaknesses

Most uncertain is ensuring the ability of these training methods to change employee behavior, attitude, knowledge or skill. According to the 2006 Industry Report, 14 percent of all training was delivered instructor-led from a remote location which represented a drop from 16 percent in 2005. In the 2005 study, 16 percent of all training in organizations of 100 to 499 employees used the instructor-led, remote-location model, while 22 percent of all training in organizations of ten thousand or more employees used this training approach. Larger companies have demonstrated a greater propensity to leverage their technological capabilities to deliver training to a greater number of employees, especially in topics that involve compliance and/ or regulatory issues. It seems the greatest challenge will be to expand the use of technology to include additional topics like sales and customer service training that appear to be more effectively delivered through the instructor-led classroom method.

WEB COURSES

Web courses are taught almost entirely over the Internet by content experts using online discussions, written assignments, and tests to measure learning and retention. Web courses can be prerequisites to instructor-led classroom training or interspersed with periodic instructor-led classroom meetings. Participants in web courses must be mature adult learners who are self-motivated to improve their knowledge, skills, attitudes, and behavior.

Trainees have greater freedom and flexibility to schedule their time and complete their web course assignments either on-site or off-site. Trainees who spend a great amount of time traveling or attending off-site meetings can complete web courses as long as they can maintain regular Internet access.

WEB MODULES AND PODCASTS

Web modules and podcasts consist of information (audio/video) that can be downloaded to a computer and then uploaded to a portable medium (iPod and/or MP3 player) to be watched/listened to on the go. Lectures, movies, and videos are some of the media that can be transmitted in this way. Training program lectures and/or videos can be viewed at the trainee's convenience, such as while commuting to and from work. Used with instructor-led training, web modules and podcasts free up valuable classroom time for training activities more appropriate for face-to-face interaction.

Summary

1. Evaluate the best ways to deliver training, given organizational requirements and constraints, in order to achieve program goals.

2. Review instructor competencies to determine internal and external resources that can be used to design and deliver training.

3. Examine whether using SMEs as trainers is the best approach to achieve training goals.

4. Determine whether training trainers to train employees is the most effective way to train large employees in large numbers.

5. Evaluate classroom training to determine whether instructor behavior and instruction methods are effectively facilitating change in trainee knowledge, skills, attitudes, and behaviors.

6. Assess the feasibility of using instructor-led classroom training, technology-assisted delivery, and/or a blend of both to deliver training most effectively.

CHAPTER SIX

Outsourcing: Finding the Right Training Provider

*"Change is the law of life. And those who look only
to the past or present are certain to miss the future."*
JOHN F. KENNEDY

Purpose

This chapter will enable you to accomplish the following:

- Review factors that help determine the suitability of using internal, external, or a blend of training resources
- Determine training design and delivery services that will be outsourced
- Identify sources of potential training providers, vendors, and consultants, as well as process and criteria for selecting the best candidates
- Examine off-site training program options and ways to evaluate their potential value and effectiveness

Overview

The training professional must assess their organization's internal competency to design and deliver training that meets organizational needs. Depending on the availability of internal training resources, a determination is made as to the design and delivery resources that will be procured from external sources. Training needs, program requirements and constraints are reviewed and finalized to craft request for proposals from potential providers. A ranking and selection process is used to determine providers, vendors, and/or consultants who will contract to complete the training project. Selected vendors are verified who can deliver as promised. Off-site programs are considered for satisfying specific training needs. Organizations will invest financially to satisfy their training needs by using internal resources, external resources, or a combination of both.

PUTTING COMPETENCIES TO WORK

Organizational training needs are often met by using both internal and external training resources. The 2006 Industry Report noted that 44 percent of organizations polled use external instructors to deliver some of their training and approximately 30 percent turn to external vendors for custom content development. Training professionals must assess both their organizations' internal capability to design and deliver needed training and which training must be provided by external training providers, vendors, and/or consultants.

The training professional must develop and follow search, interview, and selection processes to determine the vendor(s) best suited to the hiring organization. Training professionals can facilitate the process by accessing their professional community. The 2004 ASTD Competency Model identified networking and partnering as one of the interpersonal skills essential to the successful trainer role. The model defined this competency as "developing and using a network of collaborative relationships with internal and external contacts to leverage the workplace learning and performance strategy in a way that facilitates the accomplishments of business results." The training professional must ensure (as well as possible) selecting the correct vendor.

FINDING THE RIGHT TRAINING PROVIDER(S)

Once the determination is made to use external resources to design and/or deliver training to the organization, the training professional must revisit the organization's program requirements.

Choosing Customized vs. Custom-Designed Programs

Organizational needs will help the training professional decide whether program content should be customized and/or custom designed. Customized training tailors existing materials to meet the organization's specific needs. Custom-designed training is created specifically for the organization. Customized programs are most appropriate for general training topics such as management development, selection interviewing, and so forth. Custom-designed programs are most appropriate for knowledge and skills unique to the organization, such as product knowledge, proprietary software, and new employee orientation (NEO). NEO is a training program most likely custom-designed by the organization for its own unique uses. Ownership of customized programs is usually retained by the training provider, while ownership of custom-designed programs is retained by the organization.

Evaluating Outsourcing Options

The training professional can contract with training providers, vendors, or consultants to design and deliver training programs on almost any topic. Alternatively, organizations can contract separately for design or delivery. Pre-determining and confirming provider credibility is a critically important decision that strongly influences training program success. The trainees will consider the external resource to be an extension of the in-house training function. The hiring organization needs to carefully examine the training provider's credentials and capabilities to determine its capability to handle the project.

Experience

It is important to determine whether the vendor has undertaken a previous project similar in size, scope, and/or content. The training professional must evaluate previous work products as well as contact previous customers to review performance and evaluations. Training professionals generally do not want to use unproven vendors or vendors who have limited experience with successfully completing a similar project.

Strength

Depending on the magnitude of the project, training providers may need to expend significant up-front monetary and human resources to get the project underway. Training professionals must make sure that their provider has the financial breadth and depth to build the training program and maintain it as required by the contracting organization.

Instructional Design and Delivery

The provider must have previous experience with training programs of similar instructional design and delivery requirements. It is important to know how many times the vendor has developed a similar training program. Evidence of previously satisfied customers will reassure the contracting organization that they will be pleased with the results, too.

Work Quality

It is important to collect and analyze the process that vendors use in gathering feedback from previous customers. In addition to reviewing glowing reports from satisfied customers, ask vendors to identify the biggest complaint previous clients have expressed about them. Vendors do not like to reveal problems that previous customers have experienced, but the responses to this question can provide insight into areas that the contracting organization may want to pay special attention to.

A training provider who can point to evidence of professional recognition gains credibility. Published articles and/or research findings in trade magazines, books, or other periodicals demonstrate the vendor's high standing in the training community.

Trainer Credentials

If training will be delivered using an instructor-led classroom format, the hiring organization must determine whether the assigned trainer has the knowledge, skills, attitude, and behavior to effectively deliver the program to the target audience. Trainers come with different resumes: combinations of backgrounds as consultant, published researcher, author, and/or vendor; industry experience and/or professional association affiliations; undergraduate, graduate, and postgraduate degrees; non-profit, public service, government, or military experience. Different, previous professional roles will provide different knowledge, skill, and experience bases that often determine potential for effectiveness with different projects.

The training professional needs to evaluate whether the external trainer possesses the critical competencies necessary to deliver effective classroom training. Subject knowledge, speaking ability, enthusiasm, and classroom interpersonal skills are required.

Seeing is believing, so seeing the trainer in action prior to hiring for a project is very desirable. Attending the trainer's next presentation as a guest to evaluate fit for the assignment is possible with permission from the hosting organization. A presentation DVD can provide insight into the trainer's classroom skills and techniques. A personal recommendation from a trusted colleague gives the training professional confidence. If possible, face-to-face interviews prior to signing the contract will also help reveal whether this is the right trainer for the program.

FINDING RESOURCES

Vendor Listings

If the contracting organization will want the ability to conduct face-to-face meetings with training providers over significant time periods, it is advisable to search first within close proximity to the organization's headquarters. Face-to-face meetings are easier to arrange and less expensive when distance is minimized. Local, national, and international vendor listings can be found via buyers guides, directories, websites, trade shows, chambers of commerce, professional publications and articles, research studies, and word-of-mouth referrals. Colleagues in professional organizations, discussion list participants, and newsgroups can also be sources to uncover possible training providers.

ASTD's *Buyer's Guide & Consultant Directory* is an excellent provider source. The International Society for Performance Improvement (ISPI) publishes an annual directory of performance improvement resources and lists well credentialed vendors in its Buyers Guide section.

Although proximity is a consideration, location should not be a barrier to finding the best provider. Technology provides communication abilities that transcend state and international boundaries. Although live face-to-face meetings might prove challenging with providers headquartered many miles away, many types of projects can be successfully designed and delivered using electronic means.

Tradeshows and Conferences

Tradeshows and conferences, especially those organized by professional training organizations, are multi-day events that include presentations by practitioners, industry experts, and expositions by companies demonstrating their products and services. At these venues, training professionals in the market for a vendor can assess the field and see who might be the best fit for their project.

Industry-specific annual training conferences for such organizations as the Society for Pharmaceutical and Biotech Trainers and the Society for Insurance Trainers and Educators provide opportunities to survey potential training providers who have an industry-specific approach.

Attending such gatherings gives the training professional consumer the opportunity to see presentations delivered by practitioners who offer their latest books, instruments, research findings, and/or projects. Assessing practitioners' strengths and weaknesses can give the training professional important information about their potential compatibility with organizational needs. Visiting vendor booths, meeting company representatives, reviewing work samples, gathering marketing literature, and asking questions can help reveal whether the training provider could adequately address the organization's needs.

EVALUATING RESOURCES

After developing a potential provider list, the training professional must give each vendor finalist the same description of the training program's specifications. Some contracting organizations produce a structured Request for Proposal (RFP) to ensure that all potential providers are bidding on the same project. RFPs makes it easier to compare and choose the training vendor who will provide the best value, meeting or exceeding the contracting organization's requirements and expectations.

Narrow the field to between three and five potential vendors to receive the RFP. Reviewing returned proposals is a time-consuming process that should be reserved only for those organizations that stand a strong chance of being selected for the project. The RFP should contain the contracting organization's program requirements and constraints. RFPs usually include the following specifications;

Program Goals

Training goals should be clearly identified and communicated. Desired changes in the target audience's knowledge, skills, attitudes, and behaviors must be described in detail so the vendors can accurately propose designing programs to address needs. Evaluation methods, including post-program follow-up documentation, should also be discussed so that the vendors can identify the process(es) they will employ to determine whether training goals have been achieved.

Program Length (Hours or Days)

Program length should be determined by training goals. Organizations, however, have norms regarding the duration of instructor-led classroom training programs. Multiple full days, multiple half days, one full day, one half day, or lunch hour(s), are each potential training program lengths. e-Learning modules have different requirements that must be identified and shared with vendors. Training providers must be able to design training programs to meet organization time constraints as well as achieve training goals.

Delivery Method

Instructor-led classroom training or blended training that combines classroom instruction with technology such as self-study e-learning and/or a virtual classroom are each possibilities. Budget and hardware/software capabilities determine possibilities, since delivery methods have a direct impact on program development time, costs, and logistics. Training providers should be able to recommend and determine the best format to use.

Instructional Media

Depending on the delivery method, instructional media may need to be created to support the training effort. Materials such as facilitator guides, participant workbooks, PowerPoint presentations, computer-based training, web-based modules, and video may be employed. Types of media used will have a direct impact on development time, costs, and the organization's technological requirements and constraints. Potential providers should be able to give accurate advice on the most effective instructional media given budgetary and technology parameters.

Deliverables

The contracting organization needs to clearly communicate the tangible and intangible deliverables that will be produced prior to the program launch. Originals or masters that can be reproduced in quantity, such as camera-ready copy and/or photos, CD-ROM, video or audiotape, electronic files, and software might be part of the tangible deliverables package. Intangible deliverables could include the vendor's time delivering the program and/or consulting time either before or after the program. Vendors should be able to determine and deliver the final products and services.

Due Date

Contracting organizations need to pre-plan and accurately predict the timing of the training program's delivery to the organization. Trainee schedules, classroom availability, replacement workers (if necessary), and workload redistribution are a few of the many business issues that must be altered to accommodate a training program. Due date slippage by the training provider will cause a tremendous amount of additional work, inconvenience, disruption, and expense for the contracting organization. Missed deadlines diminish the credibility of the training effort and make the ability to achieve training goals more difficult. Training providers should be able to accurately describe a project timetable and keep to it.

Budget

Budget for the training program should be a pre-determined amount based on consideration of the organization's overall annual training budget and the budget for the specific training program included in the RFP. Considerations for projecting budget expenses were discussed in Chapter 4. The training professional must be mindful of budgeting dollars for other training program the organization intends to offer during the fiscal year that are not included in this particular RFP.

RFP Response Comparison

The training professional must compare vendor responses to one another as well as to the contracting organization's requirements to determine which one seems to be most on-target. Organizational protocol will determine the process used to rank and select the vendor.

A selection grid, the tool used in Chapter 3 to rank training needs, is useful for comparing RFP responses. By comparing vendors based on rating their ability to meet/exceed key project parameters, as seen in Figure 6.1, the training professional makes an objective determination of the best vendor for the job.

It is clear from the ranking that Vendor C would be selected for this project. Even though other vendors scored better on Budget (Vendor C's fee was higher than two others) and one other vendor (Vendor D) had better ratings on Experience with Topic and Design/Delivery, Vendor C appears to be the best overall choice.

FIGURE 6.1. VENDOR SELECTION GRID

	Budget	Previous Experience with Topic	Previous Experience with Design/ Delivery	Other's Recommendations	Total
Vendor A	4	2	2	3	11
Vendor B	3	3	2	3	11
Vendor C	2	4	4	5	14
Vendor D	1	5	5	1	12

1 = Lowest Rating   5 = Highest Rating

Once ranking is completed, the next step is to examine the top-rated vendor in-depth to confirm that he or she is worthy of selection. The training professional needs to ensure, as well as possible, that the vendor is willing and able to meet the project requirements committed to in the RFP.

OFF-SITE TRAINING

Perhaps fulfilling the organization's training needs includes sending certain target audiences to off-site training programs. These programs are conducted by a variety of organizational types, such as training vendors, product vendors, professional or government organizations, sanctioning or accreditation organizations, annual professional conferences, or law firms. Product manufacturers offer training in product knowledge, marketing, sales, and customer service to their clients. The training professional must determine the off-site sources that are the right training providers to satisfy training needs.

Training's goal is to facilitate knowledge, skills, attitude, and behavioral change so the trainees are better able to do their jobs and contribute to organizational goals. The training professional's challenge is to determine whether a particular external program will achieve the desired outcomes, given the investment in trainee time and expense to attend the off-site program. Examine key pieces of information prior to sending employees to external training programs to determine whether the training program will produce the desired result. The printed or electronic program brochure, announcement, invitation, or catalog should be starting point for the training professional to make an informed buy or no-buy decision.

Agenda

The program agenda describes the topic areas that will be presented. Assuming the published agenda is accurate, the topics to be addressed should match the particular learning needs of the participants. The number of topics to be covered should be appropriate to the time allocation as well.

An overly broad and ambitious agenda with many topics listed, given the amount of training time, probably means the treatment of each topic will most certainly be cursory. If this is the case, the bulk of the learning will probably rely on the self-motivated efforts of the training participant(s) to review the resource materials (such as compact discs and workbooks) that are included with the training once they return to the workplace. Perhaps the resource materials are not included in the training tuition but instead are available only for an additional cost. These details could determine the off-site program's potential effectiveness, cost-efficiency, and whether or not to send trainee(s) to attend.

Goals

Off-site training program materials should contain goal statements, written assurance that, by the end of the training program, participants will gain specific knowledge or skill(s), and/or be capable of making behavioral changes. Such statements should flow from the program topic agenda. It is the responsibility of the trainees to invest the time and effort necessary to absorb the information and demonstrate the changes once they return to work. But it is also the responsibility of the training provider to clearly advertise the program's goals and deliver on them so that everyone knows the desired outcome ahead of time. It is difficult for the consumer organization to make an informed purchasing decision if the program's goals are not clearly stated.

Reputation

Previous performance usually indicates future performance. The provider organization's reputation for training quality is an indication of the experience that trainees will probably encounter. The training professional's personal experiences as well as testimonials from trusted colleagues are perhaps the most important indicators of whether the organization should send trainees to the off-site program. Some factors that determine the perception of training quality experience are subjective and open to interpretation. But some are more objective, such as covering the agenda in its entirety, achieving stated program goals, usefulness of supporting resource materials, trainer effectiveness, and the perception that the training's cost was worth the investment.

Presenter(s)

The quality of an off-site training experience will be greatly influenced by the trainer(s) conducting the program. Familiarity and/or history with the quality of the training staff should help guide the training professional's buying decision. Personal experiences as well as testimonials from trusted colleagues can also indicate whether the trainer(s) will be able to achieve training program goals. Determining whether the trainer(s) possess knowledge of the subject, good speaking ability, and enthusiasm for the subject will help indicate their effectiveness. The training professional must ensure that the off-site presenter(s) demonstrate these crucial competencies.

The trainers' names and credentials are often listed in the program materials. These should be evaluated by the training professional to see whether their qualifications appear to make them a credible resource for your trainees. Sometimes a statement is contained in the program materials announcing the trainers for the program as well as a disclaimer that says the program will be presented by that person "or by another highly qualified member of our staff." It may be worthwhile to ensure the advertised trainer will be the presenting trainer, because this person is a key component in the quality of the program.

Budget

All decisions to send employees to off-site programs are predicated on the belief that the training budget can accommodate the cost. This option is not available if budgeted resources are not available. Off-site program expenses need to be carefully calculated. Cost and logistics go together: travel expenses and overnight accommodations (if necessary) ratchet up training program cost significantly. Off-site training is much less expensive if the program is offered locally and requires little travel and no overnight hotel rooms. Tuition and per diem food allowances are generally not affected by the location of the program. Many training vendors tour their programs throughout the country, so training can be arranged at a closer location to minimize travel, expense, and time away from the worksite.

Time

Training programs are usually offered in half-day, full-day, or multiple-day options. The number of hours an organization is willing to devote to training usually correlates to past practice and budgetary considerations. One hopes the training time is managed efficiently for a maximum learning experience. However, it is reasonable to presume that less training time usually means less opportunity for knowledge and skill improvement to occur. Achieving training goals takes a significant amount of time so a shorter training session usually means that fewer goals will be reached.

Certification and Continuing Education Units

An important factor to consider when choosing a particular off-site training program or venue is the possibility of trainees receiving credits and/or certification from the relevant accrediting agency, organization, or vendor. Many employee classifications (such as allied health professionals and information technology specialists) must attain a certain number of continuing education units (CEUs) and/or certifications within a specific time period in order to maintain proper licensure, continue practicing, or remain up-to-date professionally. A training vendor who offers certification and/or CEUs is a plus for trainees and their employers to satisfy this professional requirement, but certification and CEUs alone do not necessarily guarantee a high-quality training provider.

No matter the particular presenter, venue, cost/logistical convenience, or certification opportunity, the topic(s) presented must correlate with the organization's training priorities so the changes in knowledge, skills, attitudes, and behavior contribute to achieving strategic goals. Even the best-presented training program from a top-notch presenter misses the mark if the resultant changes don't accomplish that aim.

OUTSOURCING TRAINING NEEDS: TWO CASE STUDIES

Small Business Outsources All Training

A multi-office audiology practice in Southern California meets its training needs by using external training resources 100 percent of the time. The business owners recognize that their company's mission and strategic goal accomplishment depends on their human resources continually maintaining and acquiring knowledge, skill, attitudes, and behaviors to achieve exceptional job performance. Since each job classification in the organization has different focal points, training needs and sources to address them vary accordingly.

Overall, the organization's annual training expenditure is less than 1 percent of annual payroll. The master's- and doctoral-degree-level audiology employees, whose main responsibility is diagnosing hearing loss and recommending and dispensing hearing aids where indicated, have an ongoing need for training in the latest product technology. Manufacturers conduct regular training programs (usually one-day, instructor-led classroom sessions) at their corporate headquarters that the audiology staff attend.

Audiologists also attend professional, multi-day conferences throughout the year organized by the professional organizations with which they are affiliated. Researchers present their latest studies, vendors display their products at booths and exhibitions, and attendees meet informally with each other to discuss the latest developments in their field. CEUs are provided, which must be accumulated by audiologists on an annual basis to maintain licensure.

The office manager has ongoing training needs that reflect the multifaceted aspects of her job, and she too receives training from external resources 100 percent of the time. Handling insurance claims effectively is a key result area (see Chapter 2) that is challenging because of changing federal and state government regulation and insurance company policies and procedures. The practice's insurance agency is a member of a national organization that sponsors half-day and one-day instructor-led, classroom training sessions on proper insurance handling practices. As administrative staff supervisor, the office manager attends off-site, instructor-led classroom training programs provided by vendors on subjects like managing receptionists, conducting selection interviews, and effective performance appraisals.

The instrument specialists troubleshoot and (if possible) fix hearing aids that are brought in because they are not working. They often deal directly with patients, explaining the problem and recommending solutions. They also discuss warranty information, if appropriate.

The practice purchased an off-the-shelf package that provided a training tutorial for instrument specialists. The package included a series of learning modules on CD and DVD, along with participant workbooks. The specialists progressed through each module at their own pace, using a computer at work. The training content included instruction on how to troubleshoot problems with hearing aids and how to fix them when possible. The specialists needed to answer 100 percent of the multiple-choice questions correctly at the end of each section to proceed to the next module. The supervising audiologist reinforced the self-paced learning process by observing the specialists' work performance, providing feedback, and being available for questions when necessary.

The first two days of employment for each new receptionist consists of on-the-job training with the office manager. Policies, procedures, forms, scheduling systems, and product familiarity are some of the topics covered. A portion of each regularly scheduled all-staff meeting is devoted to a product in-service training session conducted by one of the staff audiologists. Receptionists also periodically attend one-day, off-site, instructor-led classroom training programs provided by training vendor organizations on subjects such as dealing with difficult customers and proper phone and business etiquette.

Once per year, the entire organization closes for one day and all staff attend an all-day team-building session facilitated by an external training vendor. The agenda includes a review of the vision, mission, and strategic goals; current challenges and strategies; and future goals and action plans

Large Organization Outsources Some Training

The University of California San Diego employs approximately 26,000 people. Staff Education and Development, a separate department within Human Resources, consisting of a director, three trainers, and four administrative staff, has the responsibility to offer and deliver training to all employees. Training is offered through programs in a combination of media: instructor-led classroom training, videos and video broadcasts, self-study CD-ROMs and DVDs, and web-based training.

In 2006, 216 course titles were taught in classroom-led training by 178 different instructors. Courses were offered within curriculum groups including:

1. Management and Leadership
2. Supervision
3. Communication
4. Training and Career Development
5. Environment, Health, and Safety
6. Financial Tools and Practices: Management
7. Financial Tool and Practices: Fiscal Support
8. Sponsored Projects Administration
9. Information Technology
10. Student Services

For example, courses within the Management and Leadership curriculum include Common Leadership Challenges, Performance Management, and The Practice of Listening. Courses within the Information Technology curriculum are grouped into Basics, Word Processing, Spreadsheet Management, Ergonomics, Database Management, Presentation/Print/Publication Development, Electronic Mail/Scheduling, and Web Design and Development.

The instructors included trainers from Staff Education and Development, a plethora of SMEs from several campus departments, and consultants who were contracted to design and conduct training on select topics. Classrooms were equipped to receive and play videos, closed-circuit broadcasts and webcasts. Separate computer and information technology classrooms housed networked personal computers for trainees' hands-on practice and a projection system connected to the instructor's PC. Videos, CD-ROMs, DVDs, and web courses could be accessed at work, from home, or from other remote sites. Employees also accessed training off-site by attending professional conferences and vendor-sponsored workshops.

Mix and Match

Training professionals mix internal and external design and delivery sources to match their organizations' training needs, requirements and constraints, and preferences. For outsourced assistance, they select among a group of providers, vendors, and consultants they feel will do the best job. The result is that organizational training needs are addressed by a blend of delivery media providing content focused on particular topics, all aimed at improving trainee skills, attitudes, and on-the-job performance behavior.

As previously cited, University of California San Diego (UCSD) is an organization whose training professional mixes internal and external design and delivery sources to match the organization's training needs, requirements and constraints, and preferences. The internal training staff conducts training and coaches the SMEs on training design and delivery strategies. External consultants design and conduct training programs on topics such as career development and writing skills. Self-directed learning resources, such as a self-study library containing videos, CD-ROMs, and DVDs, are provided, the availability of web-based training on selected topics, and the ability for staff to access off-site training allows UCSD to respond to its training needs by mixing and matching needs with internal and external resources.

Regardless of the design and delivery methods used, organizations need to ensure that training goals are being met. A thorough evaluation process, discussed in the next chapter, will reveal training's impact and value.

Summary

1. Assess the organization's internal competency to design and deliver needed training.

2. Determine design and delivery resources that will be procured externally.

3. Review training needs, program requirements and constraints, and preferences to craft a request for proposal process for potential providers.

4. Conduct a selection process to determine providers, vendors, and/or consultants that will contract to complete the project.

5. Verify that the selected vendor can deliver as promised.

6. Assess the effectiveness and efficiency of sending employees to off-site programs for specific training needs.

7. Recognize that organizations will satisfy their training needs by using internal resources, external resources, or a combination of both.

CHAPTER SEVEN

EVALUATION PART 1: HOW DID THE TRAINING GO?

"The secret to change is to focus all of your energy, not on fighting the old, but on building the new."
SOCRATES

PURPOSE

This chapter will enable you to accomplish the following:

- Define evaluation
- Examine responsibility for evaluation from different organizational perspectives
- Describe four types of evaluation criteria
- Examine data collection necessities and difficulties
- Examine evaluation data from a case study

OVERVIEW

The training program has been conducted, and all seems to have gone reasonably well. This conclusion is difficult to confirm with certainty unless an evaluation process documents the training program's impact. Without evaluation, there is no way to know whether trainee knowledge, skills, attitudes, and behaviors have changed because of their training participation. Organizations often fail to train effectively because they don't have the evaluation mechanisms in place to recognize that training goals are not being achieved and so the program needs to be changed. They don't have the data on which to base decisions for changing training to make it more effective.

Because organizations, large and small, spend billions of dollars annually on training, they need to know whether their investments are producing a reasonable return. The only way to reach objective conclusions regarding training's impact is to engage in a comprehensive evaluation process.

Responsibility for evaluation will be examined from different organizational perspectives. This chapter delineates Donald Kirkpatrick's widely respected model that describes four levels of evaluation criteria; reviews tools to collect evaluation data and measure impact at each level; and also examines the data's value as well as the challenges involved in collecting it. A representative case study describes the evaluation process to determine whether a training program's goal has been achieved.

How Did the Training Go?

Such a simple question to ask—and yet such a difficult question to answer accurately. "How did the training go?" is another way of asking whether the program was effective. Effectiveness is measured by evaluation, the process of determining value. Determining training's value has tremendous implications for the organization's training efforts. Comprehensive evaluation data is vital in deciding the kind and content of the training that will be offered in the future.

Responsibility for Training Evaluation

Traditionally, training evaluation has been left to the training professional. W. Leslie Rae, who has written more than thirty books on training and the evaluation of learning, proposes in *Assessing the Value of Your Training* (2002) that a "training evaluation quintet" in which each member has specific roles and responsibilities to perform that will ensure a comprehensive evaluation process.

Senior Management

Senior management must:

1. Adopt the mindset that the need and value for evaluating training is both necessary and valuable
2. Require that evaluation be conducted for each training program offered, that summary data reports are prepared, and that reports are reviewed and discussed on a regular basis
3. Include the training professional in meetings and discussions about training evaluation information and decisions that will be made based on evaluation data

Trainer

The trainer must:

1. Identify the trainees baseline knowledge, skill, attitudes and behavior data that the training program is attempting to change
2. Provide a training program that gives trainees the opportunity to learn and achieve the program's goals
3. Monitor learning as the program progresses
4. Generate and receive data on learning levels achieved by trainees by the end of the program.

Trainees' Managers

The trainee's manager must:

1. Be involved in pre-training evaluation development by providing baseline pre-program data on trainee knowledge, skills, attitudes, and behavior change related to the training topic
2. Debrief the trainees after training to discuss, agree and/or modify action plans to implement new knowledge, skills, attitudes and behaviors
3. Observe, document, and forward evidence of behavior change where applicable to the training manager to tabulate organization-wide data

Training Manager

The training manager must:

1. Maintain and bolster interest in training evaluation with senior management
2. Plan and implement the evaluation process and ensure its execution by the trainers
3. Produce regular evaluation reports for senior management and review the results with them on a regular basis
4. Act as the liaison with the trainee's manager to ensure that the manager documents and compiles data related to changes in trainee attitudes and behavior.

Trainees

Although the principal role of the trainee is to learn, the trainee must be involved with the evaluation process whenever possible. Without their comments and insights, the evaluation process is unlikely to be accurate. Trainees can

1. Provide input to the trainer on the best way(s) to collect learning data
2. Recommend to their manager how to collect information regarding pre- and post-training knowledge, skill, attitude, and behavior changes
3. Document environmental factors that will either facilitate or prevent them from implementing their newly acquired skills in their work roles

All members of the quintet have a vested interest in an effective, accurate, and comprehensive evaluation process. If any quintet members step back from any of their prescribed evaluation responsibilities, the value of the process and the significant investment that has been made in training will diminish. The overall evaluation process should avoid the look and feel of a paper-chase, number-crunching, or feel-good exercise.

For example, training is proceeding at Status Quo Organization. Approximately 2 percent of annual payroll (not including benefits and taxes) is invested in training each year. All training hours are tracked, and each employee on average attends thirty-five training hours per calendar year. Training is provided by both internal and external resources and delivered in instructor-led classrooms, self-paced e-learning, and attendance in off-site programs. Everyone seems pleased with the training program; no complaints have been lodged with the training manager.

Reaction forms are distributed and completed at the end of each on-site training program. There is 100 percent compliance with employees enrolling in training required by state and federal licensing and credentialing organizations, but less than 50 percent participate in training programs they are scheduled to attend. The training department meets its budgeted expense line.

Upon closer examination, it is revealed that:

1. Reaction form data is not compiled, analyzed, or reported to management.
2. Potential learning, behavior, or productivity gains attributable to training are not captured.
3. Off-site programs attended by employees are not evaluated by attendees.
4. Use of self-paced training tools is not tracked.
5. Management is unaware of the effectiveness, efficiency, and volume of training activity.
6. Managers routinely reschedule employees out of training programs to meet work deadlines and/or avoid staffing issues.
7. A training needs assessment has not been conducted in five years.

There is much work needing to be done to realize the full return on the organization's training investment. Status Quo Organization must have the

1. Training manager compile, analyze, and report reaction data to senior management on a regular basis.
2. Training manager and trainers expand evaluation levels to assess changes in learning, behavior and job performance results.
3. Trainees provide written feedback regarding their reactions after attending off-site training programs.

4. Trainees' managers and the training manager track the use and completion of self-paced training modules and tools.
5. Training manager publicize and regularly report training activities and results to the trainees managers and senior management.
6. Senior management team insist that the trainees managers commit to allowing trainees to attend training when scheduled without exception.
7. Training manager initiate a training needs assessment.

Each member of the training quintet must understand the importance of their roles and the reasons for what they are being asked to do.

Evaluation Methods

Donald Kirkpatrick is professor emeritus at the University of Wisconsin, where he received his BA, MBA, and Ph.D. degrees. He first proposed his ideas regarding training evaluation in 1959 in a series of articles published in *Training and Development Journal.* The articles were included in Kirkpatrick's book *Evaluating Training Programs* (1975) published by ASTD, which he had served as president. His theory has become the most widely used and popular model for evaluating training and learning. Kirkpatrick's four levels of training evaluation, later reprinted, redefined and updated in *Evaluating Training Programs* (2006) includes:

- Level 1. Reaction—the trainee's thoughts and feelings about the training
- Level II. Learning—the trainee's resulting increase in knowledge
- Level III. Behavior—the trainee's transfer of newly acquired knowledge, skills, attitudes and behavior to the work environment
- Level IV. Results—the trainee's effect on the work environment

Kirkpatrick's model states that evaluation should always begin with Level I. As time and budget allow, the process should move sequentially through Levels II, III, and IV. Findings from each prior level serve as a basis for the next evaluation level, so each successive level represents a more precise and complete measure of training program effectiveness. Each successive evaluation level, while incrementally uncovering more useful information, also requires more rigorous and time-consuming data collection and analysis process.

Reaction

Reaction describes how trainees felt about the program, including their personal reactions to the training experience. Evaluation at this level seeks trainee's answers to questions such as:

- Did they enjoy the training program (or experience)?
- Were they satisfied?
- Did they consider it relevant?
- Was it a good use of time?
- Did they like the presenter?
- Did they like the content?
- Did they learn?
- Will they apply anything from the training to their work?

Participants can provide feedback on these and other questions to the training professional through several methods:

- Written feedback forms completed at the training's conclusion
- Verbal reactions to questions that are noted for later review
- Written post-training feedback forms or online surveys
- Verbal reactions given by trainees to their managers

These trainee reactions are the first indication of the program's effectiveness.

Strengths. The beauty of reaction data is that it can be collected immediately once the training ends. All trainees are readily available so the information is relatively easy to obtain from 100 percent of the attendees. Feedback is collected through relatively simple means so it is not expensive to gather and analyze. Reaction forms completed anonymously by trainees encourages honest comments. If the feedback is complimentary, it gives the trainer confidence that the program produced a positive first impression that will most likely be shared with the next trainee group.

Weaknesses. Others think reaction data is misleading. A study by George Alliger entitled "A Meta-Analysis of the Relations Among Training Criteria" (1989) indicated an exceedingly weak correlation between reaction and other evaluation criteria (that will be reviewed later in this chapter). In other words, positive reactions do not necessarily mean that attendees experienced intended benefits from the training. Richard Clark, a professor of educational psychology and technology at the Rossier School of Education at the University of Southern California and his co-author Fred Estes go even further to debunk the value of reaction data in their book *Turning Research into Results: A Guide to Selecting the Right Performance Solutions* (2002). They state that people like training programs more when they learn almost nothing and tend to dislike courses when they learn a lot. Perhaps it has something to do with the discomfort that change in knowledge and skills (and resultant attitudes and behavior) produces in some people, especially those with high levels of denial and resistance in the first place.

Learning

Learning measures the change in acquired knowledge that occurs from pre- to post-training. Evaluation at this level seeks trainees answers to questions such as:

- Did they learn what they were supposed to learn?
- How much knowledge did they gain compared to the knowledge they were expected to gain?

Learning is usually assessed by comparing scores on topic-related instruments and/or tests administered before and after training. Measurement and analysis is more easily conducted on a group scale when tests are given to all trainees at the beginning and end of a classroom training experience. Hard-copy, electronic, and/or online formats are all possible. Establishing reliable, clear, scoring measurements will minimize the risk of inconsistent or misinterpreted results. Pre- and post-training interviews with trainees and/or observations of them can be collected and analyzed as well.

Strengths. Liking and learning are not necessarily correlated, so making assumptions about training impact based solely on reaction may not be a wise strategy. Learning is a stepping stone to skills, attitude, and behavioral change; documenting trainee knowledge acquisition usually signifies a subsequent report of potentially positive training impact. Conversely, measuring knowledge and uncovering gaps helps pinpoint areas that must be addressed. Overall, it is usually good for both employees and for the organization when trainees learn through training. It is also fair to say that it is good for the training professional to strive for and measure this change if and when it occurs. Evaluation mechanisms to measure learning such as what training participants knew before (pre-test) and after (post-test) attending training can be relatively simple to implement but require more thought than reaction-level evaluation. Such data is highly relevant to the training topic, clearly delineated, and quantifiable.

Weaknesses. Poorly designed systems and processes to capture learning data will increase the cost and time that are required to measure and analyze information. Also, learning's direct effect on specific behavioral change can be less easy to quantify. For example, it is challenging to assess what behavioral change (if any) will be seen in trainees who acquire product knowledge as a result of participating in product knowledge training. If the trainees were customer service representatives, one goal would be that they could now answer customer questions more quickly and accurately. If the trainees were salespeople, one goal would be that they could now overcome customer objections more easily and/or be perceived as more knowledgeable by the customer. Learning is a stepping stone to behavior change, but does not ensure it.

Behavior

Behavior measures the extent to which trainees apply their newly acquired knowledge to change their behavior. Evaluation at this level seeks trainees answers to questions such as:

- Did they put their learning into effect when they returned to work?
- Was their relevant knowledge and skill used?

- Did they demonstrate noticeable and measurable change in activity and work performance when back in role?
- Was the change sustained over time?
- Would they be able to transfer their learning to another person?
- Are they aware of their change in knowledge, skill, and behavior?

Assessing whether behavioral change has occurred requires regular, subtle, and ongoing observation and interview by an external source over a period of time. Data then needs to be transferred to a suitable analytic tool for further study in order to reduce the observer's natural subjectivity. The trainees' opinions of their own behavior change is relevant but highly subjective and unreliable and needs to be buttressed by other data. Feedback using a 360-degree approach is a useful way to augment the trainees' self-opinions. With 360-degree feedback (signifying the complete circle of people working around the trainee) trainees receive pre- and post-training behavioral feedback from all employees who work with and observe the trainees' behavior. Arbitrary snapshot assessments are not reliable indicators because people change behavior at different times in different ways that can only be captured by ongoing observation, reporting, and analysis.

Strengths. Data-collecting instruments and processes for behavioral evaluations, designed around key result and performance areas, produce findings that are more meaningful (that is, more clearly linked to goal achievement) than reaction and learning data. Behavioral observations can be integrated into existing performance management systems and serve to strengthen the breadth and depth of feedback provided by the organization. Self-assessment can be useful as long as carefully designed criteria and measurements are used and augmented with a team approach (that is, 360-degree feedback) to observe and document behavior change. Using this method contributes to a supportive work environment that encourages and rewards peers helping peers for the betterment of the department and ultimately the entire organization.

Weaknesses. Accurately measuring behavioral change is more difficult to quantify and interpret than both reaction and learning evaluation methods. Some in the organization will question whether the necessary time and labor-intensive expense of capturing pre- and post-training behavioral data is justified. Simple and quick data collection processes are unlikely to be adequate. Cooperative, skilled, and relatively objective observers (and trainees) are necessary, but they are difficult variables to control. Managing and analyzing ongoing, subtle, behavioral assessments on a large scale is a challenging assignment. Online and electronic data collection methods can be more difficult to incorporate into existing structures.

Evaluating whether behavioral change has occurred is an extremely important yet challenging assessment to make. Documenting favorable reaction to training and trainee learning contributes little to the organization if concurrent changes in trainee behavior back at the job are realized but not reported.

Results

Results measure the effect on the organization and/or work environment that the trainee's improved job performance causes. Evaluation at this level seeks answers to trainees' questions such as:

- What changes in results are attributable to training-related improved job performance?
- Which result measures are already in place only requiring a link to training input?
- Which result measures might need to be created to accommodate their newfound output?

Results that are produced because trainees have improved job performance usually fall along key departmental and/or enterprise-wide goals such as improved productivity, less waste, lower costs, more deadlines met, reduced accidents, fewer customer complaints, higher quality ratings, sales growth, greater employee satisfaction, and customer retention. Collecting training related results information usually represents an overlay with normal, good management practice. All that might be necessary is linking training activities to regular data collecting processes.

Strengths. Quantifying and analyzing improved job performance results that can be solely attributed to the training program provides a significant basis for determining training's return on investment (ROI). Comparing pre- and post-training productivity for each trainee in key result areas is not difficult if systems (such as standards of job performance) and monitoring procedures are already in place to capture this data. Annual performance appraisals can be structured to measure and reward the individual trainee's impact on business results in key result areas.

Kirkpatrick and other theorists have referred to ROI as perhaps a fifth evaluation level. Others include it as an extension of Level IV results evaluation. Training ROI will be discussed in the next chapter.

Gathering results data to assess training's financial value is not a new endeavor. A great example of a results-oriented training evaluation process was reported in an early study (1953) published in *Personnel Psychology* by Wallace and Twitchell and cited in 1972 by Bass and Barrett in *Man, Work, and Organizations*. The study reported that the amount of life insurance sold by salespeople tends to decline after year one. The study found that after four years 52 percent of Canadian insurance agents were selling 10 percent less than in their first year, while only 29 percent of this sample of 243 agents were selling more. Another group of 230 insurance salespeople underwent three four-week classroom training periods at Purdue University and carried out training assignments on the job for the remainder of the year. A control group that did not receive training was matched with each of the 230 training program attendees for aptitude, sales volume, marital status, and age. The production by salespeople in the control group decreased by 10 percent per month for the one-year study. By contrast, the production by salespeople who had participated in the training rose by 23 percent for that same one year following training. It is clear that through a training evaluation process that focused on results, a determination could be made that the training program had a positive impact on the organization's strategic goals for increased sales.

Weaknesses. Having the ability to measure the trainee's post-training impact on the organization and/or work environment assumes that the organization already has systems in place to measure job performance in key result areas. This is not always the case. It is difficult, if not impossible, to measure training's impact after the fact when systems are not in place to collect baseline (pre-training) job performance data. Conducting results evaluation across the entire organization is very challenging due to scale and constantly changing job structures, roles, and responsibilities. Linking training impact to bottom-line results changes can be elusive. External factors can greatly influence enterprise-wide and/ or departmental performance that have little to do with changes to trainee behavior. Demonstrating cause-and-effect relationships between training and improved job performance results can often be a challenging proposition.

For example, XYZ Hospital regularly sends its receptionists to training for handling difficult visitors and phone calls. Receptionist reactions to the training (via evaluation forms) have been favorable, and learning instruments completed before and after the training indicate that trainees are absorbing knowledge. Feedback from co-workers indicates that, after attending training, the receptionists appear to be calmer when dealing with irate visitors and phone calls. However, visitor complaint data maintained hospital-wide indicates no appreciable decrease in complaints against receptionists has been noticed since the training began.

This case illustrates the numerous issues that often make tracking results data difficult. Complaints lodged against receptionists don't always include names; therefore it is difficult to determine whether the receptionist being cited has been trained or not. The hospital occasionally employs temporary workers to fill in for receptionists when regular employees are sick or on vacation; complaints lodged against receptionists could be the temporary workers who are not training recipients. Not all less-than-satisfactory interactions between employee and receptionist are documented; hospital-wide visitor complaints may be less than accurate. These reasons illustrate the difficulties encountered in linking training impact to bottom-line results.

Difficulties and Necessities of Data Collection

Training professionals appreciate evaluation's importance to the entire training process. Evaluation data is vital to determining whether the training effort has addressed issues uncovered in the original training needs assessment. It becomes more meaningful and useful when, according to Kirkpatrick, each evaluation level builds on the previous one.

Examining the data collecting process shows that it is increasingly more difficult to collect data at each subsequent evaluation level: reaction data is easiest to capture, followed by learning and behavior; results data is most difficult to document. Not surprisingly, evaluation data beyond reaction is collected less frequently. Catalanello and Kirkpatrick reported in the *Training and Development Journal* (1968) that 77 percent of a national sample of training directors used reaction data as a criterion for measuring training effects, while only 46 percent used results data. ASTD's *2005 State of the Industry Report* reported that 91.3 percent of their respondents evaluate their training programs at Level I, 53.9 percent evaluate at Level II, 22.9 percent evaluate at Level III, and 7.4 percent evaluate at Level IV.

On the other hand, training professionals appear to spend significant time trying to improve evaluation efforts. The ASTD 2004 Competency Study found that survey respondents spend 7.6 percent of their time measuring and evaluating training. More specifically, they gather data to answer questions regarding the value or impact of training; focus on the impact of individual programs to create overall measures of system effectiveness; and leverage findings to increase effectiveness and provide recommendations for change.

Recent data, reported in the ASTD *2005 State of the Industry Report,* indicates that training professionals collect learning, behavior and results-oriented evaluation data far less often than reaction data. Many explanations are possible for this trend. Collecting in-depth evaluation data is a resource-intensive process requiring time and people skilled in this procedure, two resources often in short supply in many organizations. Organizations seem generally satisfied with training professionals whose priority and performance provide the desired training (programs). Evaluating training program effectiveness beyond reaction is usually viewed as a nice-to-have, not a must-have, and so it is done infrequently. If training is conducted on-site by an external trainer or by sending employees to off-site programs, the likelihood of collecting evaluation data diminishes even more. Training is assumed to be successful as long as trainees react favorably to the training program as indicated by reaction data.

But training success is measured by people changing their knowledge, skill, attitudes, and behavior so they can perform their jobs more effectively and be more likely to achieve their goals, their departments' goals, and the organization's goals. It is risky to assume that trainees' positive reactions to training programs results in learning, behavioral change, and improved job performance in key result areas.

The training professional cannot safely assume, for example, that sales training participants who reacted favorably to sales training are now selling more; that customer service people who reacted favorably to customer service training are providing better customer service; or that interviewers are conducting better interviews and selecting better candidates because they enjoyed selection interview training.

Ideally, the training professional should institute, at minimum, a Level I evaluation process and then make every attempt to build on each subsequent level, collecting data from each of the four evaluation criteria. If using all four criteria is not possible, then using one level (reaction) or two levels (reaction and learning) or three levels (reaction, learning, and behavior) is preferred. Even using only reaction data can still give the training professional important evaluative information.

The outcome of a comprehensive evaluation process also gives the training professional the opportunity to present important information to the decision-makers who endorsed the training effort in the beginning and to publicize successes to training's stakeholders and trainees. Stakeholders refers to all groups who might be affected by training's actions and successes, including employees, customers, investors, board of directors, stockholders, donors, and suppliers. Documenting and providing a full array of aggregated evaluation data, including reaction summaries, learning improvements, behavioral changes, and/or performance data reinforces the perception that training is a positive organizational force, a well-placed investment with tangible returns. The training professional hopes the outcomes have met expectations, but even if they haven't met every goal, the results will likely demonstrate that training processes can facilitate needed changes that support the mission and purpose of the organization. A more complete discussion related to promoting training's successes will be reviewed in Chapter 9.

Evaluating a Training Program: A Case Study

It is not uncommon to predicate a training program's success on influencing behavioral choices the trainee says they will display if/or when confronted with a specific situation. For instance, one goal of safety training would be that "by the end of this training, participants will be more likely to follow proper safety procedures in the event that a fire is observed in the workplace." A pre- and post-training questionnaire completed by trainees could ascertain their likelihood to follow these procedures and thus see whether the desired change in preferred behavior had been achieved.

Sexual harassment prevention training defines sexual harassing behavior for trainees and sends the message that it is unwarranted, illegal, and will not be tolerated by the organization. Additionally, information is usually presented instructing trainees to take appropriate action (such as talk with a manager and/or consult human resources) if they experience sexual harassment. Stated in SMART terms (see Chapter 4), "By the end of this training, participants will be more likely to contact a manager or human resources if they feel they are being sexually harassed as measured by trainee ratings on a pre and post training assessment instrument." A second SMART goal would state: "By the end of this training, participants will be less likely to ignore sexual harassment behavior as measured by trainee ratings on a pre- and post-training assessment instrument." The following case study examines efforts to evaluate the success of achieving these two goals.

Data Collection

A total of 687 people were surveyed before and after attending a two-hour sexual harassment prevention training program to determine the action they would pursue if they felt sexually harassed. Training program participants were mixed groups of males and females, managers and non-managers, from all departments of several different organizations. Group sizes ranged from fifteen to fifty attendees. All training programs had identical topic agendas. At each training session, after introductory remarks, the facilitator would make the following statement to the group:

"Assume for a moment that you currently feel you are being sexually harassed at work. On a scale of 1 to 5, with 1 being highly unlikely and 5 being highly likely, write on the blank piece of paper in front of you the probability that you would take each of the following six actions: (1) talk to a manager (assuming he or she is not the harasser); (2) report the incident to human resources; (3) contact an attorney; (4) confront the harasser; (5) ignore the behavior; or (6) discuss the incident with a co-worker."

Trainees were asked not to put their names on their papers to maintain anonymity and confidentiality. Trainees then attended a two-hour instructor-led sexual harassment prevention classroom training program. At the conclusion of the two-hour session, just before distributing reaction evaluation sheets, the trainees were asked to take out the piece of paper they had previously completed and revisit their answers to the hypothetical situation: What would they do if they felt they were being sexually harassed at work? They were asked to write their new (post-training) 1 to 5 ratings for each action next to their original (pre-training) rating, even if it was the same as their original response. All papers were collected.

DATA RESULTS AND ANALYSIS

All trainee pre- and post-training mean scores for each action were compiled and analyzed for statistically significant differences. Statistically significant differences would indicate divergence that is not likely the result of a random event.

For the option *talking to a manager* (Figure 7.1), the mean pre-training rating was 3.4, as compared to a mean post- training rating of 3.7, a statistically significant change at $p < 0.001$.

For the option *reporting the incident to human resources* (Figure 7.2), the mean pre-training rating was 3.1, as compared to a mean post-training rating of 3.7, a statistically significant change at $p < 0.001$.

FIGURE 7.1.   GROUP AVERAGE FOR ACTION 1

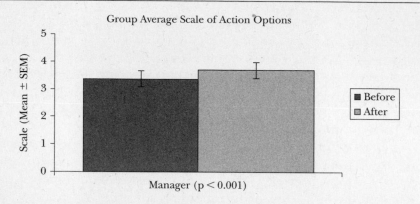

FIGURE 7.2.   GROUP AVERAGE FOR ACTION 2

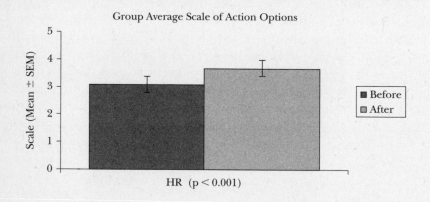

For the option *contacting an attorney* (Figure 7.3), the mean pre-training rating was 1.8, as compared to a mean post-training rating of 2.0, a statistically significant change at $p < 0.01$.

For the option *confronting the harasser* (Figure 7.4), the mean pre-training rating was 3.8, as compared to a mean post-training rating of 4.0, a statistically significant change at $p < 0.001$.

For the option *ignoring the behavior* (Figure 7.5), the mean pre-training rating was 2.5, as compared to a mean post-training rating of 2.2, a statistically significant change at $p < 0.001$.

FIGURE 7.3. GROUP AVERAGE FOR ACTION 3

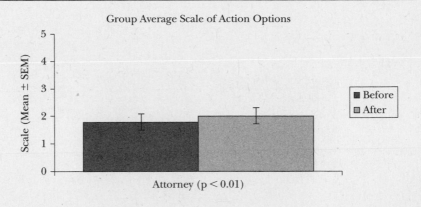

Group Average Scale of Action Options

Attorney (p < 0.01)

FIGURE 7.4. GROUP AVERAGE FOR ACTION 4

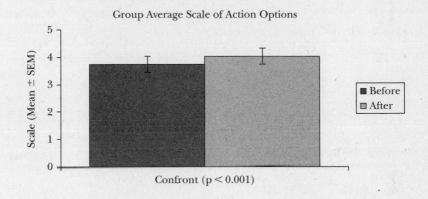

Group Average Scale of Action Options

Confront (p < 0.001)

FIGURE 7.5. GROUP AVERAGE FOR ACTION 5

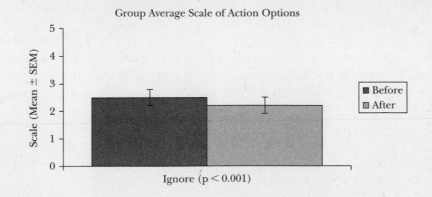

Group Average Scale of Action Options

Ignore (p < 0.001)

FIGURE 7.6. GROUP AVERAGE FOR ACTION 6

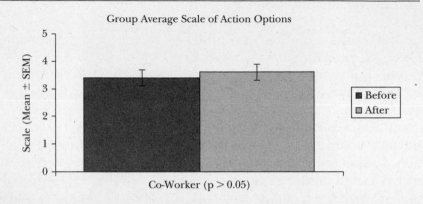

For the option *discussing with a co-worker* (Figure 7.6), the mean pre-training rating was 3.4, as compared to a mean post-training rating of 3.6, a statistically significant change at $p < .05$.

DISCUSSION

Before attending sexual harassment prevention training, trainees anticipated that if they were confronted with sexually harassing behavior, they would respond, in descending order of preference, in the following ways:

1. Confront the harasser
2. Report the incident to human resources
3. Discuss with a manager or co-worker (tie)
4. Ignore the behavior
5. Contact an attorney

After attending the training, trainees anticipated that if they were confronted with sexually harassing behavior, they would respond, in descending order of preference, in the following ways:

1. Confront the harasser
2. Talk with a manager or report the incident to human resources (tie)
3. Discuss with a co-worker

4. Ignore the behavior
5. Contact an attorney

Using the criterion of self-reported anticipated behavior, Level III according to the Kirkpatrick Evaluation Model, the results indicated that the training program achieved the goal of increasing the likelihood that trainees would contact a manager and/or human resources if sexually harassed. The training program also achieved the goal of decreasing the likelihood that trainees would ignore sexually harassing behavior. Level 1 reaction data was collected, analyzed, but not reported; it was determined that trainees had overwhelmingly positive feedback related to their overall impression of the training, the presenter, and the practicality of the information. Level II learning data was not collected, nor was Level IV results data. Level III data was viewed as most relevant in this case.

Unexpectedly, trainees reported with statistical significance that their first choice was to confront the harasser, a preference that was a consistent finding with both the pre- and post-training assessment. Confronting the harasser is an option rarely discussed, much less encouraged in sexual harassment prevention training.

EVALUATION PROCESS RAISES QUESTIONS

When the evaluation process raises unexpected questions, it is imperative that the training professional pursue the finding(s) to see where they may lead. In this case, the training professional unexpectedly found that trainees would prefer to confront their harasser. If this were the finding within a single organization, the training professional, in discussion with human resources, should weigh the proposition that employees, if they so desire, should have the opportunity to confront their harassers.

The irony is that guidelines from the Equal Employment Opportunity Commission, the federal agency responsible for enforcing laws regarding sexual harassment, states that "It is helpful for the victim to inform the harasser directly that the conduct is unwelcome and must stop." Current sexual harassment training does not typically encourage or include tips for trainees to confront sexual harassers directly. The subject is certainly one for further discussion.

The evaluation process hopefully finds positive trainee reactions, learning gains, desired behavioral change, and improved job performance results. If the evaluation process uncovers less than satisfactory feedback, the training professional has the information necessary to make needed changes to the training program to improve outcomes. The next chapter will examine a further delineation of the evaluation process that helps determine training's value in financial terms.

Summary

1. The training professional must collect data to determine the training program's impact on trainees knowledge, skills, attitudes, and behavior.

2. Although the training professional is ultimately responsible for an effective evaluation process, others in the organization play significant roles in supporting the effort.

3. Donald Kirkpatrick's four-tiered evaluation model is the most widely respected and used evaluation model in the field.

4. Evaluation data builds from each successive tier, although data gathered at each subsequent level is increasingly valuable and difficult to obtain.

5. The evaluation process can uncover unexpected findings that may have unintended implications for the organization.

CHAPTER EIGHT

EVALUATION PART 2: IS TRAINING ADDING VALUE?

"It is not the strongest of the species that survive, nor the most intelligent, but the one most responsive to change."
CHARLES DARWIN

PURPOSE

This chapter will enable you to accomplish the following:

- Examine processes for calculating training's value
- Learn about a return on investment (ROI) methodology that calculates training's costs and benefits in dollars and cents terms
- Examine learning analytics, a process that organizes raw training evaluation data into a format of actionable information
- Explore additional tools that a training professional can use to evaluate training, such as online surveys, data marts, and digital dashboards that convert large amounts of relational data into easy-to-grasp formats so that decision makers can make more informed decisions

OVERVIEW

Training professionals face a daunting task when they attempt to assign value to training. Accurately calculating expenses and return on an organization's training investment is an exhaustive process that reaps great rewards when properly executed. This chapter examines evaluation models and technology-assisted evaluation that can demonstrate training's value to the organization in terms that everyone understands—dollars and cents.

Determining Training's Value

The question "How did the training go?" is being replaced more frequently with the question: "Is training worth the expense?" With organizations in the United States spending billions annually on training, it seems reasonable that the professionals responsible for the effort are more frequently asked to calculate training's dollars-and-cents value.

The focus on accountability has also been encouraged by recent study results. A 1999 ASTD report offered definitive evidence that increasing investment in training improves profits and *total shareholder return* (TSR). The study ranked 2,500 corporations on how much they spent on training, and the results showed that organizations in the top half of the ranking realized a TSR that was 86 percent higher than those in the bottom half.

Perception of Value Varies by Position in the Organization

Training's value is often defined by the person's position in the organization. The training professional's goal is to close the knowledge/skill/attitude/behavior gap between actual and desired job performance, as indicated in the initial training needs assessment. The trainer will see value in positive changes in trainee job performance. The department manager's goal is to achieve departmental goals. The manager wants training to help meet or exceed performance targets projected for the work unit. The senior management team wants to fulfill the organization's mission and vision and gain a competitive advantage. Management wants training to improve enterprise-wide results and equate training's value with adding shareholder value.

Kirkpatrick's Evaluation Model Enhancement: ROI

Attempting to determine training's value in dollars and cents is a challenging but not a new phenomenon. Training's value, according to Kirkpatrick's evaluation model developed in the

1960s and discussed in Chapter 7, is determined by assessing each of four progressively in-depth evaluation levels: reaction, learning, behavior, and results.

Some experts believe that a Level V evaluation, *return on investment* (ROI), is a subset of Level IV results and does not warrant a separate level. Other professionals, namely Dr. Jack Phillips, claim that ROI is a separate evaluation level that compares training program benefits to costs.

Phillips is chairman of the ROI Institute, an organization established in 2003 and based in Birmingham, Alabama. The Institute strives to assist professionals in improving their programs and processes by using the ROI Methodology. Phillips is a world-renowned expert on accountability, measurement, and evaluation. He received his undergraduate degrees in electrical engineering, physics, and mathematics and a master's degree in decision sciences from Georgia State University. He received his Ph.D. in human resource management from the University of Alabama. Dr. Phillips developed the ROI Methodology in the 1970s, published his first study, Measuring the ROI in a Cooperative Education Program, for Lockheed-Martin in 1973, and has authored ten books on the subject.

While all evaluation data has value when analyzed and used for making decisions to improve training, a more in-depth evaluation process will yield more useful information. ROI information is deemed more valuable than data generated through Levels I, II, III, and IV for several reasons. While reaction data seeks to identify training consumer preferences, ROI data seeks to quantify training's benefits to those who fund, support, and approve the effort. Not surprising, Level I evaluation data is the easiest to access and is collected most frequently, estimated by the ASTD *2005 State of the Industry Report* to be gathered 91 percent of the time training is conducted. Level V evaluation data is the most difficult to access and is collected least frequently. Phillips estimates that ROI analysis is implemented between 5 percent and 10 percent of the time due to expensive and resource intensive data-collection methods.

ROI Methodology

Phillips' ROI method involves applying financial metrics to the data collected from each of the four levels of evaluation in

Kirkpatrick's model (learner reaction, learning, job behavior, enterprise-wide results) and applying them to a formula that calculates return on investment.

1. Assign a financial value to difficult-to-quantify intangible benefits such as increased job satisfaction, commitment to the organization, improved teamwork, positive reactions to training, learning gains, and reductions in complaints, conflicts, and stress levels.
2. Calculate a financial value for other benefits derived from the training program such as Kirkpatrick's Level IV results.
3. Compute training program costs. These costs generally include instructor or facilitator fees; content development, training materials, facilities; travel/lodging/meals/refreshments, training department salaries and benefits, participant salaries and benefits; and training administrative and/or overhead costs.
4. Determine a benefit/cost ratio (BCR) by dividing total program benefits by total program costs:

BCR = Total Program Benefits/Total Program Costs

5. Determine ROI by dividing net program benefits (total program benefits − total program costs) by total program costs:

ROI = Net Program Benefits/Total Program Costs

An ROI Example

After conducting a training needs assessment, an organization determined that outdated and ingrained business processes barred it from achieving its strategic goals. The training manager recommended, with the approval of senior management, instituting a continuous process of review and improvement. During Phase 1 certain employee groups were trained in selected topics related to total quality management. After one year, the organization decided to do an ROI analysis to see whether the initiative should be expanded in the second year to include additional employee groups.

The first-year training program costs totaled $100,000, including trainee salaries and benefits, instructor or facilitator fees, program design and material costs, administrative or over-head costs, training supplies, and refreshments. First-year training program benefits totaled $350,000, resulting largely from process improvements that included time saved in streamlining customer acquisition and problem-solving processes, creation of paperless supply ordering processes, and improved troubleshooting and response-to-problem processes. Intangible benefits including reported increased job satisfaction, organizational commitment, teamwork, and customer satisfaction were also factored into the calculation.

$$BCR = \text{Total Program Benefits/Total Program Costs}$$
$$= \$350,000/\$100,000 = 3.5 \text{ or } (3.5:1)$$

$$ROI = \text{Net Program Benefits/Total Program Costs}$$
$$= \$350,000 - \$100,000 = 2.5 \text{ or } 250 \text{ Percent}$$

An ROI of 250 percent means that for each $1 invested, there is a return of $2.50 in net benefits after costs are accounted for. The organization decided to expand the continuous process review and improvement effort in the second year to include all employees.

Benefits of the ROI Methodology

The difficulty in collecting Level V data, according to Phillips and other ROI advocates, is offset by its numerous benefits.

Aligns Training with Organizational Need. Effective training is all about deploying resources to achieve organizational goals. Determining ROI for programs focused on the organization's training needs demonstrates training's alignment with, and investment in, enterprise-wide efforts to support goal achievement. Revisiting the training needs assessment that uncovered the original training need and the knowledge, skills, attitudes, and behavior that the training aimed to change supports the notion that the return on training investment is being applied to high priority training programs.

Determines Individual Training Program Contributions. ROI analysis allows training professionals to determine the bottom-line contribution that each training program produces. Once ROI is calculated, senior management can identify the programs that demonstrate the greatest return on investment and make decisions such as to expand the program's target audience and/or increase the organization's investment in specific training programs.

Conversely, the programs that demonstrate the weakest return on investment can be examined more closely to determine the cause of the outcome. Decisions can be made to either redesign the program to make it more cost-effective or eliminate the program and shift investments to programs that produce a greater yield.

Earns Senior Management Respect. ROI analysis helps earn senior management respect because training is expected to be accountable for its activities. Linking training with bottom-line performance improvements means more executives expect training to be run as a business. Donna Goldwasser, senior editor for *Training* magazine, says that executives now expect traditional, "soft" training metrics (such as reaction summaries and learning improvements) to be accompanied by more direct proof of training's value to the organization in terms of dollars and cents

Justifies Budget Expense. Training has long been regarded as a necessary, unavoidable expense that flew under the radar of organizational accountability. The ROI Methodology gives training professionals the opportunity to justify budget expenses by demonstrating financial benefits that organizations receive from training.

When resources shrink or business downturns occur, organizations are compelled to look for ways to reduce spending. Training departments, like all departments, have been the target of budget cuts. Phillips' ROI Methodology gives budget-cutting decision-makers another metric to consider: Cutting the training budget may also mean reducing financial returns on the training investment.

Improves Support for Training. Those in the organization who viewed training skeptically as a department that spent funds without accountability may change their opinions when ROI is calculated. Armed with powerful data, training professionals can publicize ROI results to senior management, department managers, supervisors, and non-supervisory employees to clearly show the positive financial impact that training produces. Stakeholders will be more likely to support training when they know that the effort they are investing in is yielding a significant return on the organization's dollar.

Isolates Training's Effects. A critical step in the ROI process is isolating training outcomes from other factors that influence output. One or more techniques, such as use of control groups, separate out non-training related factors from ROI calculations. For example, if customer satisfaction levels spike after a customer service training program, the improvements may have been caused—at least in part—by other factors such as cyclical patterns, a new customer promotional program, or a new sales campaign not related to the training. The ROI model requires that all potential contributing factors be identified and accounted for to determine the precise effect of training on investment return.

ROI at Its Best

Phillips states that his ROI Methodology should be implemented selectively as a process improvement tool and not as a performance evaluation tool for the training department. Determining ROI strengthens and improves the training process. It provides its greatest value to the organization when it is applied to training programs that are

1. Critically important to supporting organizational goals;
2. Costly and highly visible with large target audiences; and
3. In which management is strongly interested.

Under these conditions, ROI findings make the greatest impact on both training activities and the decision-makers who shape training's organizational role.

ROI CHALLENGES

Investment or the cost of training may be easier to identify than its return or benefit. Assigning value to trainee-reported changes like improved job satisfaction, increased organizational commitment, reduced stress, better time management, and enhanced teamwork in dollars and cents is tricky. Isolating these changes to one training experience can also be difficult to support. Some say training ROI assessments should be thought of as estimated, not absolute, financial calculations.

It is not accidental that Level V evaluation is conducted least frequently than the other four levels. It is the most difficult, time-consuming evaluation process. The training professional must be convinced that calculating ROI benefits outweigh the labor-intensive process, and that the information derived will be worth the extra effort.

For the trainer, the dialogue has shifted from the generic "How did the training go?" to the more specific "What value did the training bring to the organization?" Whether the evaluation process includes any or all Levels I, II, III, IV, or V, the attention to measurement can only help make training a more valuable organizational contributor. What's important, says *Training* magazine's Goldwasser, is that a business value has been attached to the training experience. "By attempting to measure value—by any means—we can't help but promote its existence."

Learning Analytics

In short, learning analytics studies the impact of training on trainees. The training professional's challenge is greater than simply ensuring that the target audience is exposed to learning activities. The organization needs to ensure that the right knowledge, skills, and competencies are acquired. Top-performing organizations seek to understand the economics of their training initiatives and to leverage that understanding to create efficient and effective programs and processes that will make them market leaders. They seek to measure learning results using the same process in place to determine strategic goal performance. The training professional's goal is to quantify the ROI of learning in terms that are understood by stakeholders (internal to the organization) and shareholders (external to the organization). The ability to report on the effectiveness of training programs has become increasingly mandatory, as both stakeholders and shareholders demand accountability for the organization's efforts to leverage training to its greatest advantage.

The Need to Know

Senior management teams, focused on achieving enterprise-wide strategic goals, need to know how specific initiatives will determine their success:

- Does our sales force know enough to sell our new product lines better than the competition can sell theirs?
- Have our employees received training required to comply with government regulations?
- Do our employees know how to access information about our products or services so they can adequately inform customers and differentiate us from our competitors?
- Do our non-employee strategic partners in the field have the knowledge, skills, attitudes, and behavior to properly represent our organization to customers?

Customer education is a major contributor to revenue and profit. Employees armed with the proper knowledge, skills, and competencies to deliver this vital information have the greatest potential to contribute to the organization's strategic goals. The senior management team has a profound need to know that this is occurring.

The Connection: Enterprise-Wide Results with Learning Data

Organizations have made great advances in generating large amounts of data about their strategic goal accomplishment and about their training programs. The challenge continues to be to demonstrate the connection between trainee learning and their ensuing contribution to strategic goal achievement, the ROI that results from training.

To that end, training professionals try to answer such critical questions as:

- Which departments use training most or least and what impact does that use or nonuse have on trainee job performance?
- Which training topics are most effective?

- Which training (instructor-led classroom type as well as e-learning) programs are generating the greatest results, and which are generating the poorest results, in terms of trainee reaction, learning, behavior, results and ROI?
- Which programs should be expanded and which should be dropped?
- Which department managers use the most or least training resources? How do their departments' performance metrics compare?
- What is our training ROI on a program-by-program basis? Which should be expanded and which should be eliminated to reduce expenses without diminishing program quality?
- Is the organization complying with mandatory government training requirements?
- Which departments and/or managers are meeting or not meeting expectations?

Leading organizations now team training professionals with department managers to create a set of learning metrics that are used to set standards and expectations for training resources utilization and optimization.

Application of Kirkpatrick's Evaluation Level 3 and Level 4

Measuring training evaluation at Kirkpatrick's Level III (behavior applied on the job) and Level IV (impact on enterprise-wide results) occurs respectively in only 22.9 percent and 7.4 percent of the organizations surveyed, according to the ASTD *2005 State of the Industry Report.* Apparently, this level of evaluation has proven too difficult (costly? time-consuming?) for most training professionals to undertake. The need to compare training data to enterprise-wide performance data in order to create objective measures of training's organizational impact (combining and standardizing data from many different sources) stretches beyond the borders typically undertaken by training professionals.

Analytics represents the discipline of correlating and analyzing large amounts of data that originate from diverse and divergent locations in order to identify trends and opportunities for innovation and mission critical strategic improvement. With analytics, organizations can create metrics that determine whether causal relationships exist between training efforts they make toward achieving objectives and the results they produce. Just as enterprises have learned to measure sales and marketing program effectiveness, it is now possible to measure training's effectiveness in producing results. Training recipients can be connected to improved business results by correlating knowledge, skill, attitude, and behavior acquisition with achievement of enterprise-wide strategic goals. Even one step further, analytics provide the organization with the ability to visibly observe the impact of their training investment on areas such as compliance, effectiveness, efficiency, revenue, and costs.

System Requirements

The essence of an effective analytics system is its ability to distill a dizzying amount of data into actionable information. It is a conduit to data that is otherwise hidden from view. It must be user-friendly, so it becomes an instant addition to the training professional's decision support infrastructure. It must allow for out-of-the-box analyses that are not predetermined. The system should include intuitive and efficient data-sharing capabilities so, for example, department managers and senior managers can monitor operations directly from their e-mail boxes. The system's architecture should be scalable to an enterprise-wide level so that the amount of data to be processed does not fundamentally limit the value of the system.

Analysis Possibilities

While it is impossible to predict all the possible analyses that a team of senior managers, department managers, and training professionals would strive to achieve, the following areas should be addressed:

Training Topic Use
Determine levels of use by training topic to identify areas for which additional investment might be justified and current costs

might be reduced. Resulting actions will improve the efficiency of the training program.

Training Activity

Identify departments that use training and those that do not and correlate this data with departmental goal achievement. Resulting actions will increase access to training for underperforming departments.

Regulatory Compliance

Identify departments that have participated in compliance programs. Resulting actions will assess departments that have greater or lesser exposure and generate action to mitigate risk.

Resource Use

Evaluate the efficiency of resource use to determine the most and least useful resources. Resulting action plans will identify trends in resource use and generate plans to use resources more efficiently.

Financial Analysis

Assess the true total cost of training programs and their use by different departments. Resulting action plans will ensure that use and future budget allocation are appropriate.

Vendor Analysis

Evaluate use of training vendor offerings (both off-the-shelf and off-site) to determine cost-per-trainee, trainee satisfaction, learning gains, and improved job performance. Resulting action plans will ensure greater use of vendors who achieve high levels of trainee satisfaction, low cost-per-trainee investment, learning gains, and improved job performance.

e-Learning Analysis

Compare the use of e-learning training with instructor-led, classroom training to determine cost-per-trainee, trainee satisfaction, and knowledge/skill/attitude/behavioral transference to on-the-job results. Resulting action plans will match training offerings with the most efficient and effective delivery systems.

AN EFFICIENT PROCESS

Most organizations struggle with the process of identifying training's impact on strategic organizational goals. Since there is a time lag between analyzing and correlating data and reporting results, traditional reporting systems tell what happened in the past, but not what is currently happening. Analytics identify what is happening, why it is happening, and immediate actions that can be taken to create continuous improvement.

Immediate access to correlated information improves training operations, reduces costs, allows more efficient use of training vendors, ensures compliance, and improves training's overall impact on enterprise-wide operations. It allows senior management, department managers, and training professionals to all receive actionable information that is linked to the common goal of leveraging training to achieve maximum organizational performance.

AN EXAMPLE: ANALYTICS IN ACTION

A training professional wants to analyze a new sexual harassment prevention training initiative that has been rolled out to the organization. The government requires that all employees in a supervisory role receive a minimum of two hours of interactive training on the topic at least once every two years. More than one thousand individuals must comply by the end of next quarter. Individuals must complete either an instructor-led classroom option or a self-paced e-learning module, both of which are available. The training professional decides that he wants to view the following:

1. Number of trainees attending each classroom session to see whether the facilitator is training close to the one-hundred-seat room capacity.
2. Number of trainees yet to be trained from each department to check manager compliance with the initiative to train all supervisors and managers by end of next quarter.
3. Number of trainees using the classroom option and the self-paced option to see whether both should continue to be offered.
4. Learning retention using the two delivery options to see whether one approach has better learning gain than the other.

5. Total cost of the program so an ROI analysis can be performed at a future date.
6. Trainee satisfaction with each delivery option to determine ongoing use.

Analytics determined that the classroom was never more than 54 percent filled to capacity for any training session. Action was taken to schedule fewer sessions (saving facilitator fees) and enrollment per session grew to 86 percent capacity.

Only 47 percent of Mary Contrary's managers and supervisors had completed the program, while no other manager had a compliance rate lower than 75 percent. The training professional sent an e-mail to Mary (with a copy to her manager) letting her know of the discrepancy. Within two weeks, Mary's compliance numbers had jumped to 80 percent, the same compliance number as her peers.

About the same number of managers and supervisors are using classroom and self-paced training. With an 86 percent classroom capacity rate, cost per trainee for either option is the same. Reaction data indicates that trainees are equally satisfied with both learning options. Since post-training retesting indicates that learning retention is the same for classroom and self-paced trainees, it appears that both delivery options will be kept.

An ROI analysis will be performed at a future date when the cost of the training program can be compared with the (hopefully) reduced number of sexual-harassment-related complaints, investigations, and lawsuits.

Technology-Assisted Evaluation

Evaluation requires data. Technology can provide great assistance in generating and correlating data that supports the evaluation process. Online surveys, data marts, and digital dashboards are three tools used to assist organizations in evaluating their training methods.

Online Surveys

Online surveys are structured interviews in which questions are displayed online. Responses by survey participants are recorded for the evaluator to analyze.

Much can be learned from online survey responses that aid the training evaluation process. Surveys can be constructed to ask questions regarding:

1. Trainee reactions to training programs
2. Assessment of program content
3. Presenter competencies (for instructor-led classroom training)
4. Quality of learning activities
5. Relevance or usefulness of the training program

The trainee reactions to these questions help determine changes to future training programs.

Online surveys can also be used to help determine trainee knowledge retention. Questionnaires that relate to the training topic can be distributed to participants weeks and/or months after they have attended a training program to see which questions (and what percentage of questions) are answered correctly. Knowledge erosion can point to needs for retraining as well as topics that have to be covered.

Online survey questions can ask trainees to self-report on behavioral change they have experienced since completing training. Surveys can also be distributed to receive 360-degree feedback from others about the trainees' post-training behavioral change. The evaluator can analyze this data to determine the trainees' apparent behavioral change resulting from the training program.

Online Survey Characteristics

The evaluator's goal is to achieve a 100 percent return rate with online surveys. Analyzing training data is most effective when most (if not all) trainees respond. The survey should be short— ten questions or fewer. The survey must be in an easy format should take only take five or ten minutes for users to complete. If it's too long, they will not respond. A mix of closed (multiple-choice) and open-ended questions is suggested. Closed questions are easier to analyze; open-ended questions, while more difficult to analyze, may provide richer data.

Two examples of closed questions are:

My overall impression of the trainer was favorable.   Yes   No
I found the training program useful.   Yes   No

Two examples of open questions are:

What was most beneficial about the training? Please comment.
How would you have liked the training done differently? Please
    comment.

A two-tiered survey process is possible. The first survey tier, as
described above, is short and easy to respond to. On that survey,
ask whether the trainee is willing and interested in completing a
survey with more in-depth questions. If so, the respondent then
proceeds to a more in-depth second-tier survey at the conclusion
of the first. In this way, the evaluator can capture more in-depth
information without risking a low response rate by subjecting all
responders to more in-depth questions in the first tier. The evaluator must expect that only a small percentage of all respondents
will probably proceed to the second tier.

Capturing Pre- and Post-Training Data

Evaluation is the process of determining training's value or
effectiveness for the purpose of making decisions. Capturing
pre- and/or post-training data using online survey methodology
provides information to the evaluator that would otherwise be
unattainable.

Reaction surveys and learning instruments completed during
the training program assess trainee attitudes and knowledge during the experience. Online surveys allow evaluators to capture
data both before and after training has been completed and provides the opportunity to compare it to the data collected during
the training.

Online surveys completed pre-training allow evaluators to
determine how much information trainees know before the
program. In-class surveys indicate knowledge gains attributable
to the training program. Online surveys completed post-training
indicate knowledge that has been retained. Scores from post-
training surveys that fall below a certain level can indicate the
need for retraining.

Trainee behavioral data can be captured via an online survey.
A self-report as well as feedback from others can be compiled and
tabulated through a pre-training online survey. The online survey
process can be repeated post-training, and the information that

is compiled and tabulated can indicate behavioral changes that the training program produced. Online surveys conducted weeks and/or months after training can indicate whether behavioral changes produced by training have continued to be manifested at work.

DATA MARTS

A data mart is a specialized version of a data warehouse. It is similar to comparing a supermarket with a distribution center. Data marts contain a subset of operational data that helps decision-makers to strategize based on analyses of past trends and experiences. A data mart is predicated on a specific, predefined need for a certain grouping and configuration of select data. The configuration emphasizes easy access to relevant information.

Organizations typically have multiple data marts, each one relevant to one or more departments for which it was designed. Data marts may or may not be dependent or related to other data marts in the organization.

If the data marts are designed to use shared facts, dimensions, and assumptions, then they will be related and interdependent. Training data marts typically incorporate data that is present across the enterprise.

In some applications, each department is the owner of the data mart, including all the hardware, software, and data. This enables each department to use, manipulate, and develop its data as appropriate to departmental needs. In this model, data marts do not interact with each other and so altering one data mart does not alter information inside others or inside the data warehouse.

A data mart is a decision-making tool that provides easy access to frequently needed data. It creates the ability for a group of data users to collectively view the same information and thus improve their problem-solving and decision-making response time. It is lower in cost than implementing a full data warehouse. Potential data mart users are more clearly defined in a data warehouse. Data marts allow end-users to manipulate their data without interfering or depending on the centralized data warehouse to manage that workload. For security purposes, data marts selectively separate an authorized data subset for viewing by a select group of end-users.

Data marts can provide a proving ground that demonstrates the viability and ROI potential (of training) prior to migrating it to the data warehouse.

DIGITAL DASHBOARDS

The digital dashboard is a business management tool used to visually ascertain the status of an enterprise by viewing year-to-date strategic goal accomplishment in real-time. Based on the metaphor of the instrument panel in a car, digital dashboards use visual, at-a-glance data displays pulled from disparate business indicators to provide warnings, action notices, next steps, and summaries of business conditions. They are intended to give decision-makers the input necessary to drive the business. Devices such as red or green or yellow lights, alerts, drill-downs, summaries, and graphics with pie charts and bar charts highlight the visual display. Users can see high-level processes and then drill down using pre-programmed menus into lower-level data.

Three main types of dashboard dominate the market: stand-alone software applications, web-browser-based applications, and desktop applications. Specialized dashboards track all enterprise-wide functions, including human resources, recruiting, sales, operations, security, information technology, project management, customer service, and many others. Departments are the end-users and information technology is the enabler. The effective use of digital dashboards is based on relying on the correct choice of metrics to monitor.

History

Digital dashboards began to be developed in the 1970s. Most systems were developed in-house by organizations to consolidate and display data that was already being gathered in various information systems throughout the organization. The goal was to provide information to decision-makers that supported fast and accurate internal decision-making processes. With the surge of the World Wide Web in the 1990s, digital dashboards as we know them today began to appear. Today, digital dashboard technology is available off the shelf, but certain companies still continue to develop and maintain their dashboard applications in-house.

Benefits

Digital dashboards allow end-users to view how well each department is doing in relation to its performance metrics. They gauge how well an organization is performing overall by allowing the end-user to capture and report specific data points from each department within the enterprise, thus providing a snapshot of enterprise-wide performance. The visual presentation of performance measures make them quick and easy to assimilate. Management can identify and deal with negative trends immediately. Detailed reports can be generated when new trends emerge. More informed discussions and decisions can be made based on collected and shared information. Real-time information helps to make adjustments where necessary in order to align strategies with organizational goals.

Training Content

Human resource dashboards usually have a training component. While the metrics that are tracked and reported vary according to the enterprise and the preferences of the end-user, typical training metrics include the following items:

1. Percent of employees or managers who report that training has improved work performance
2. Percent of employees involved in training and development plans
3. Percent of employees who achieve development plan objectives
4. Average dollars spent on employee training
5. Percent of planned training activities that develop predetermined competencies.

Summary

1. Training's value can be calculated by assigning a dollar value to the data uncovered within each of Kirkpatrick's four evaluation levels.

2. A return on investment (ROI) methodology, advocated by Dr. Jack Phillips, attempts to calculate training's costs and benefits in dollars and cents.

3. Learning analytics attempts to organize raw training evaluation data and create an output of actionable information.

4. Additional evaluation tools, such as online surveys, data marts, and digital dashboards, help make large amounts of relational data available in easy-to-grasp formats for decision-makers to make more informed decisions.

CHAPTER NINE

ENSURING AND PROMOTING TRAINING SUCCESS

"We must become the change we want to see."
MAHATMA GHANDI

PURPOSE

This chapter will enable you to accomplish the following:

- Present recommendations to decision-makers to gain approval to proceed
- Market the training program internally to the entire organization
- Publicize success to employees, stakeholders, and customers
- Conduct a training audit

OVERVIEW

Once all of the key processes have been completed, the training professional is ready to present recommendations to the decision-makers for rolling out the training program to the organization. After receiving permission to proceed, the training professional must then launch an internal marketing campaign to the entire organization that brings everyone up-to-date on the forthcoming training program. Once it's underway, it is crucial to collect and analyze evaluation data and publicize successes to employees, stakeholders, and customers. Conducting regularly scheduled training audits helps keep effective training processes in place and changes practices that need alteration.

Getting Ready to Market

Let's assume that each step in the training process has been completed: needs assessment data has been compiled, analyzed, categorized, and prioritized; design and delivery options have been explored and decided on; budgets have been formulated; evaluation processes, tools, and techniques are in place. Before launching the training effort, depending on the organization's normal processes, the training professional should seek and receive (in)formal approval by a manager or group, such as the senior management team, to proceed. Meeting with the appropriate individual(s) to review and discuss plans prior to rollout serves many purposes. It's one last opportunity for the decision-maker(s) to ask questions and provide input on multifaceted aspects of the training effort. It's also an opportunity to confirm their buy-in, support, and involvement with the proposed program. Seizing this and other opportunities to market the training program internally is a useful way to create anticipation and engagement with the training effort. Effectively pre-selling the training product/service with potential customers (that is, employees/trainees) will go a long way toward breaking down barriers to change and readying the audience for the training experience when it's made available.

For training to accomplish its primary goal of facilitating change in trainee knowledge, skills, attitudes, and behaviors, it must take on the attributes of any successful product and/or service: it must appeal to (and satisfy) the ongoing needs of its users or customers. It is helpful for the training professional to think of the overall training effort as a product and/or service that must be embraced by all internal customers, employees at all organizational levels.

Approval Meeting

At minimum, the training professional should address several key points when meeting with the approving body. Address questions as to the "who, what, when where, why, and how" of the training effort (although not necessarily presented in that order) gleaned mainly from needs assessment results, along with other key pieces of information. The training professional hopes all in attendance are of the mindset that training's goal is to help the organization achieve its mission and strategic objectives and that implementing the suggested recommendations will fulfill this purpose. Address the following key points:

Why is training prescribed? Training's purpose is to change employee knowledge, skill, attitude, and behavior. Needs assessment results would have indicated that training would achieve job performance improvements, having a positive impact on the organization's strategic goals. It may be worthwhile to summarize the comprehensive training needs assessment process that was conducted, including the data collection methods that were used, such as interviews, surveys, and other reports, and the numbers of people and job categories that provided input.

What topics and information will be covered? Distributing and discussing the selection grid (see Chapter 6) with all potential topics identified alongside their strategic goal impact, provides the rationale for the training program topics selected. The training professional must be as certain as possible that the selection grid is an accurate representation of the organization's training priorities. The training professional does not want the approving body to review, question, discuss, and debate the ratings in the individual cells of the selection grid. If this occurs, the decision-makers are essentially telling the training professional they don't feel comfortable with the recommendations resulting from the training needs assessment process. In that case, the training professional must ascertain the source of the decision-makers' discomfort, regroup, and address those concerns before proceeding with the training program (rollout).

Recommended priority training program topics and related content reflect the knowledge and skill improvements that will have the greatest impact on strategic goal achievement. A proposed program agenda with goals should be developed and presented for each training topic offered. For example, an agenda for a product knowledge session could include information on product history, current specifications, features, warranties, troubleshooting methods, frequently asked questions, and return policies and procedures.

How will training be designed and delivered? Program content could be designed by either internal or external sources. Classroom-led instruction, e-learning/technology-assisted training, or a blend of both classroom and technology methods is possible for training delivery. Training programs could be presented by in-house trainers, other internal employees such as subject-matter experts, external consultants, or others who have the competencies to conduct a successful effort.

Who will be the training recipient(s)? Identify the target audience, including the total number of people to be trained. The training professional may recommend and discuss that it is advantageous to train certain segments of the employee population first, with other target groups to follow. For example, a greater impact on the organization's strategic goals may occur if sales and customer service employees attend product knowledge training first, followed by human resources and manufacturing staff.

When will training begin? The decision-makers will want to know the timeline for launch, for example, the third quarter of the current fiscal year. They will also want to know the approximate date by when all target audience members will have completed training e.g. the first quarter of the following fiscal year.

Where will training occur? Identify all classroom training location(s), both onsite and offsite.

What other information should be shared? Other information that can be shared at the approval meeting and other appropriate forums include annual budget projections (that is, training expenditure as a percentage of total payroll (minus benefits and taxes), training expenditure per employee, hours of training per employee, total program benefits, total program costs), plans to market the training program internally, evaluation methods and anticipated success metrics for Levels I through IV and ROI, and ways of publicizing training's successes throughout the organization.

Once the training professional receives permission to implement the training program, it is critical to communicate the training plan to the entire organization.

MARKETING TRAINING INFORMATION TO THE ENTIRE ORGANIZATION

It is important to inform all employees about the process and results of the training needs assessment, the highly ranked training topic(s), the timeline for the rollout, the involvement of the management team, and the knowledge/skill/attitude/behavior improvements that are the training program's goals. These are the people who participated in the training needs assessment via interview and/or survey, and so they will definitely want the training professional to close the loop, to tell them the assessment results and how the collected information will be used. When the next training needs assessment is conducted, employees will remember that their input was valued the previous time.

Using the appropriate organization communication channels (staff meetings, e-mail, voice mail, enterprise-wide meetings, catalogs, and/or newsletters) to tell employees about the results of the training needs assessments and the training program to follow will create positive buzz and anticipation for the training effort. A thorough and comprehensive internal marketing and communication effort will serve the training professional well when it is time to deliver the training program. Most employees will remember and understand the reasons they are attending the program and will enter the training experience with a greater likelihood of exploring change instead of resisting it or wondering where the need for the training topic originated.

PUBLICIZING TRAINING OUTCOMES TO STAKEHOLDERS

Various industry leaders are proud to report research findings to the organization's stakeholders. "Most ten-year-old cars still on the road," "highest-rated in customer service," "fewest dropped calls" are examples of what organizations say when attempting to instill the perception of product quality, value, and customer attentiveness in the hearts and minds of stakeholders, especially both potential and current consumers.

"You can't manage what you can't measure" is an old management adage. "You can't market what you don't measure" is true as well when it comes to communicating training's organizational impact. Data collection and analysis are required to make claims about training's contribution to the organization's strategic goals. Once the training program is underway, it is imperative that the training professional have the processes in place to collect evaluation-related training information on an ongoing basis. Reporting data that publicizes training's impact sends a strong message that serves many purposes. It demonstrates the organization's commitment to continuously working to maintain and improve employee knowledge and skills. It lets everyone know that the training professional is monitoring, analyzing, and reporting on specific metrics. Depending on the results, the data reported gives everyone insight into the training department's organizational impact by reporting on specific evaluation measures and outcomes.

Reaction Data

Summarizing and reporting aggregated, or total, reaction data lets everyone know how trainees are responding to the training. Depending on the questions asked, trainee feedback is being received and reported regarding the program content, instructor competency, learning activities, and other characteristics of the training. Positive reaction data from one training session will give future trainees a positive first impression of the training and confidence that the program they'll be attending will be a rewarding experience.

For example, if the answer to "Please rate the usefulness of the information presented" received an average score of 4.4 on a 5-point scale for the employees who have participated so far in a time management training program, the remaining employees will have confidence that the information to be presented in training will be useful to them as well.

Learning Data

Summarizing and reporting aggregated learning data lets everyone know whether learning is occurring during training. When a high percentage of trainee scores improve on pre- to post-training learning instruments, it indicates that trainees are acquiring knowledge, the first step toward skill, attitude, and behavioral change.

For example, if the time management training pre-test of all trainees thus far yielded an average percent correct score of 63 and a post-test yielded an average percent correct score of 81, it appears that those who have participated in the program are now more knowledgeable about effective time management techniques than they were before the training. Similarly, if it can be reported that 88 percent of the trainees' post-training scores improved over their pre-training scores, it seems that the great majority of trainees acquired knowledge. Combined with reaction data, it might be accurate to conclude that most trainees had a favorable reaction to a positive learning experience.

Behavioral Data

Summarizing and reporting aggregated behavioral data lets everyone know whether the training program is producing behavioral change. When a great majority of trainees and/or the people who observe them report frequent incidences of pre- to post-training behavioral change, it indicates that training is facilitating behavioral change.

For example, if 74 percent of the trainees who have participated thus far in a time management training program self-reported that they now spend significantly more time working on high-priority tasks and to-do items than before training, it seems that the great majority of trainees are now better time managers. Combined with reaction and learning data, it might be accurate to conclude that most trainees had a positive reaction to a learning experience that produced behavioral change.

Results Data

Summarizing and reporting aggregated results data lets everyone know whether the training program is producing results. When a great majority of trainees achieve significantly higher pre- to post-training job performance results, it indicates that training is facilitating change in job performance results.

For example, if 79 percent of the supervisors of trainees who have participated thus far in time management training report that their direct reports have gained 10 percent on their key result areas/performance indicators from pre-training levels, it seems that the great majority of time management trainees are now more productive. Combined with reaction, learning, and behavioral data, it might be accurate to conclude that most time management trainees had a positive reaction to a learning experience that produced positive behavioral change and a 10 percent increase in performance.

ROI Data

Summarizing and reporting aggregated ROI data lets everyone know the return on the organization's training investment in financial terms. When training is viewed as a sound fiscal investment in employee knowledge and skill enhancement, the effort is perceived less as a necessary expense and more as a wise deployment of resources.

For example, if the ROI of time management training is calculated to be 84 percent (meaning that $1.84 is returned for every $1.00 invested), the expense of the training program is viewed as very worthwhile. Combined with reaction, learning, behavioral, and results data, it might be accurate to conclude that most time management trainees had a positive reaction to a learning experience that produced positive behavioral change and improved job performance at a cost-effective price.

Other Metrics

Organizations report training activities using several measures. The possibilities are only limited by the organization's data-collecting capabilities and preferences. ASTD, in its *2007 State of the Industry Report*, uses investment, expenditure distribution, effectiveness, and efficiency as major categories to analyze and report training activity. Training professionals should think through their reasons for collecting and reporting various training data before proceeding. Following the metrics used by ASTD or other reporting organizations gives organizations the ability to benchmark their findings against nationwide results. Examples of training metrics tracked in various enterprises include the following:

- Training expenditure per employee
- Training hours used per employee
- Training expenditure as a percentage of total payroll (not including benefits and taxes)

- Distribution of training expenditures among internal resources, external services, and tuition reimbursement
- Number of enterprise-wide employees per training staff member
- Average cost per learning hour used
- Training hours per delivery method: instructor-led classroom, self-paced, or a blend
- Training utilization per department
- Reaction, learning, behavior, results, and ROI data per training delivery method: classroom-led instruction, self-paced, or a blend
- Reaction, learning, behavior, results, and ROI per training topic
- Percent of employees who completed mandatory compliance or regulatory training
- Number of employees trained per training staff member
- Time required for employees to achieve readiness or competence

In an increasingly competitive business environment, organizations are always looking for opportunities to leverage training. Collecting, analyzing, and reporting evaluation data and other metrics used to track the volume and performance of the training effort differentiate one enterprise, in a positive way, from another. In ASTD's *2007 State of the Industry Report*, the training performance effectiveness metric used most often was productivity improvement, followed by employee retention, quality of products and services, customer satisfaction, employee satisfaction, increase in sales and revenue, safety improvement, employee engagement, overall profitability, overall performance, and compliance.

Organizations that are willing and able to report such information to their stakeholders send the message that they are proud of their training processes and the results they produce. They are banking on the far-reaching ramifications that such a pronouncement will produce.

Employees sense WIIFM, the opportunity to develop knowledge and skills that will assist current performance and perhaps make them more competitive for other internal job opportunities.

If they feel training will be advantageous to them personally, their readiness to learn is enhanced, and they are more interested and motivated to explore training. Investors perceive that their investment will bear fruit with an organization that nurtures and grows its human resource talent. And customers hearing positive training news will be more likely to purchase a product and/or service from an organization that bluntly states that, because of its superior training processes, its employees are better trained that the employees of their competitors.

Not-So-Good Results

Undertaking an evaluation process is a calculated risk. It is not safe to assume that all training outcome data will be favorable. For example, trainees' reactions to training might be both positive and negative, learning gains not as prominent as anticipated, behavioral change bordering on inconsequential, performance results marginal, or ROI smaller than expected.

The training professional needs to ask the necessary questions and collect the required information to draw accurate, evaluative conclusions about the training program's effectiveness. There is no guarantee that favorable results will be uncovered. He or she must be prepared for the possibility that all news will not be good news.

Once the evaluative data is revealed, the training professional must deal with the results. Training professionals would probably conclude that broadcasting less-than-favorable data to stakeholders without a corrective action plan is like shooting oneself in the foot. Publicly casting dispersions on one's own training effort would seem to serve little if any productive purpose. No news about the training's impact, however, is not good news.

Evaluation in this context is the process of determining training's value and/or effectiveness for the purpose of making decisions. The training professional must deal with less-than-satisfactory evaluation data in a constructive and straightforward manner. From the onset of the training process, evaluation data (reaction, learning, behavior, results) must be analyzed for trends so that corrective changes and decisions, where necessary, can be made early on. The goal is for training to be as effective as possible so that it provides maximum value to the organization.

Collecting and analyzing actionable evaluation data and dealing with the results ensures that the training effort is fulfilling its responsibilities.

The training professional can continue to report on efficiency and volume metrics (that is, number of employees trained, investment, delivery methods) and save effectiveness data for a later date when midstream changes have taken place and effectiveness data may improve. Regardless, the training professional must let the enterprise know the activity level and resulting impact that training is having on the organization.

The Training Audit

An audit is a process normally associated with an official examination, analysis, and verification that the organization's financial matters are in proper order. Most organizations are required by federal and/or state law and/or internal bylaws to conduct financial audits annually so that government regulators, investors, and other stakeholders can gain assurance that the enterprise is fiscally healthy.

A training audit examines, analyzes, and verifies that the organization's training effort is in proper order. While few, if any, organizations are required by law to conduct training audits, they achieve a similar goal as a financial audit: They assure that the enterprise is healthy from a training point of view.

Just as a financial audit can make recommendations for changes to various accounting procedures where warranted to improve performance, a training audit can make recommendations for changes to various training processes where warranted to improve performance.

Seven Keys to an Effective Training Audit

Intentionally or not, organizations follow three different paths when it comes to their training efforts: they either provide training that is predominantly effective, provide training that is predominantly ineffective, or provide no training at all. Given the choice, employers would naturally prefer the option of providing training that is overwhelmingly effective. By conducting periodic training audits, organizations can self-assess their processes to develop action plans and implement changes to ensure that effective training will be an ongoing activity. Seven key areas to consider include the following:

1. Training Needs Identification

Does the organization have and regularly use a systematic, ongoing training needs assessment process, using either a task analysis or a strategic needs assessment method, to identify specific knowledge, skills, attitudes, and/or behaviors needing improvement?

If training needs identification processes are in place, the organization must ensure that it regularly initiates this activity on an annual or consistently scheduled basis. This way, the information generated from the assessment determines training offerings that always reflect current and high priority learning needs. One individual should be responsible to ensure and communicate that this process is conducted with information and recommendations to the decision-makers for appropriate action.

If a training needs assessment process is not in place, the organization must initiate and endorse such an activity to ensure that its training effort is aligned with the organization's strategic goals and resultant learning needs. A specific individual must own the training needs assessment process. That individual is responsible for driving the process and ensuring that the training needs information is collected, analyzed, and communicated, with recommended actions, to the decision-makers for their discussion and ultimate approval.

2. Interactive Training

Does training engage the adult learner interactively, whether in an instructor-led classroom environment, self-paced, or blended training delivery, so that knowledge, skills, attitudes, and behavioral change have a greater opportunity to occur?

If training is perceived to be adequately interactive, the organization needs to ensure that this continues to be the case, since training's overall effectiveness and value are maximized when this occurs. Continuously collecting and analyzing aggregated evaluative reaction data provided by trainees will indicate whether training is actively engaging learners.

Interactive content, delivery methods, and/or instructional techniques help engage trainees in the learning process and thus make them much more likely to explore and commit to learning initiatives and behavioral change than disengaged trainees.

If the training professional is uncertain or knows that the program is not sufficiently interactive, he or she must take action to ensure that training is adequately interactive. The first step may be to initiate the data collecting processes that ask trainees the appropriate question(s) to assess the current state. The data may indicate that changes are needed in program content, delivery method, and/or instructor technique. Regardless of the source of disengagement, corrections must be made so that training is more interactive and more effectively engages trainees. The overall training effort is generally evaluated more positively and produces greater impact when the interaction level between trainees and the training activity is high.

3. Qualified Trainers and Content Providers

Whether performed by in-house training staff, internal subject-matter experts, or external content providers and/or trainers, has a training professional reviewed and approved the qualifications and training materials of all providers to ensure that they will produce a high-quality training experience?

Even if trainers and content providers are qualified, organizations should continue to preemptively review trainer competencies and their program content to ensure continued quality control. Qualified providers are more likely to produce a training effort that achieves intended program goals.

Legal challenges to the legitimacy of the organization's training program can be thwarted by demonstrating that due diligence was followed in determining the best resources to use for a particular training initiative. On an ongoing basis, training professionals should observe training program content and delivery first-hand to ensure that trainees are being provided a quality product. This direct knowledge of training output will give the training professional ample opportunity to provide accolades and constructive feedback to the providers.

If organizations do not review the qualifications and competencies of their training content and delivery providers, they run the risk of using training resources that will not adequately support training goal achievement. Just as an employer would not hire individuals without first checking their qualifications and background, organizations should not designate individuals for training tasks without first reviewing their skills and competencies to perform satisfactorily. Observing training first-hand also gives the training professional the information needed to determine whether the provider is performing to their expectations.

4. Demonstrated Management Support

Is management clearly committed to supporting the training effort? What evidence reinforces this assumption?

If management is clearly committed to supporting the training effort, it is in everyone's best interest to make management's support visible and well-known throughout the organization. According to the ASTD *2007 State of the Industry Report*, 94.4 percent of their BEST Award Winner executives issued public statements supporting training, 89.4 percent included training objectives with performance goals, and 73.4 percent participated as an instructor or speaker. Trainees will be more likely to embrace the training effort when they know that the program enjoys management support.

Managers can clearly demonstrate their support for training in a variety of observable ways. For example, they can ensure that 100 percent of their training-eligible direct reports participate in training within the shortest period of time possible. They can conduct staff meeting discussions that specifically include training. They can develop performance evaluation goals that include training participation and consistently monitor progress toward goal completion. They are conscientious about (or have received training in) how to encourage trainees to integrate their newly learned knowledge and skill into their job performance.

If management is supportive behind-the-scenes but not publicly, a clear and public communication campaign must be mounted to demonstrate its support for the training effort. Management must (1) provide adequate financial investment; (2) communicate supportive public pronouncements; (3) link participation in training to performance expectations, (4) encourage, not impede, training participation; and (5) actively solicit trainees returning from training to apply their new-found knowledge, skill, attitude, and/or behavior on the job. If management is publicly supportive but falls short behind the scenes, the team needs to walk the talk if it wants to maximize its training investment and subsequent positive organizational impact.

The organization's employees receive a clear message from management regarding training's priority and importance. Strong public and behind-the-scenes support usually results in a training effort that flourishes; weak or no public and/or behind-the-scenes support usually results in a training effort that flounders. The opposite is rarely true; strong management support rarely produces a floundering training effort, and weak management support rarely produces a training effort that flourishes.

5. Evaluation Processes

Are evaluation processes in place and consistently used? Is action taken once evaluation data is collected and analyzed?

If evaluation processes are in place, the organization must continue to collect, analyze, and communicate the data through appropriate channels to stakeholders. Efforts should be made, if they are not already in place, to expand evaluation capabilities to include Levels I through IV (reaction, learning, behavior, and results) of Kirkpatrick's evaluation model (Chapter 7). Processes should also be instituted, if not already in place, to conduct ROI analysis when deemed necessary.

The beauty of evaluation data is that it is always actionable once it has been collected. At the very least, reaction data can serve to recognize and reward trainers and/or content developers for providing a positive training experience. Reaction data can be shared with stakeholders to publicize the trainees' positive reaction to training. Where indicated, reaction data can be used to change the training program to make it more user-friendly. At the very best, comprehensive evaluation data from Levels I through IV plus ROI can serve as the basis for a multitude of conclusions regarding training's impact on the organization's strategic goals.

There is no benefit to ignoring evaluation data. Strategies should be in place to use evaluation data to the fullest extent possible. It can be used to justify and support training to the management team by calculating and communicating its impact on strategic goals and ROI. Evaluation data may also generate excitement among prospective trainees and customers. The training professional uses the information to initiate changes that make the training effort more effective and/or efficient.

If evaluation processes are not in place, the organization needs to establish methods for collecting evaluation data, beginning with Kirkpatrick's Level I. Efforts should then be made over time to expand the reach to include progressively deeper evaluation levels.

A lack of evaluation capabilities presents a host of problems. The organization, if challenged in court, may have difficulty defending the ability of the training program to have adequately prepared employees to do their jobs effectively. Without evaluation data, the organization cannot assess training's effectiveness and cannot determine what changes, if any, are necessary to improve it. Evaluation outcomes serve as the foundation for training success; without such data there are no successes to report to stakeholders.

6. Training Database

Does a training database track targeted and actual employee participation in training programs and other vital training information? Are reports generated that communicate actionable information for decision-makers, training professionals, and managers?

If a training database is already in place, the organization must continue to track all training activities. Whether web- or server-based, training profiles established for each employee indicate programs to complete, if required, for licensing, certification, compliance, competency, and/or career development. Reports can be generated that monitor the progress of all completed and pending training for each employee grouped by department, manager, division, and/or enterprise-wide. These systems help ensure that all employees receive the training they are required and/or intended to receive in the designated time frame. Expense tracking is included in database input, assigning training costs associated with each training activity. Reports can then be run to determine training efficiencies and ROI. Legal questions regarding any employees' participation in any training activity can be easily summarized and reported.

If a training database system is not in place, the organization does not have the capability to easily track employee training activities. It will be more difficult to monitor if pending training has been completed and if employees are completing all recommended training. Actionable information is not available for decision-makers, training professionals, and managers to assess training activity. Training expense tracking is more cumbersome and inefficient, with greater likelihood of inaccuracies. Determining overall training efficiencies and ROI becomes much more difficult. Since any employee's participation in any training activity cannot be easily summarized and reported, resolving legal questions becomes a very challenging exercise.

Training tracking databases serve as the basis for determining efficiency results and are essential for documenting, communicating, supporting, and justifying the level of training activity and expenditure throughout the organization.

Without such databases in place, the organization must rely on inefficient and potentially inaccurate methods for collecting essential, training-related statistics.

7. Retraining Opportunities

Is employee retraining strongly encouraged and undertaken as needed to ensure trainees possess adequate job knowledge, skill, attitude, and behavior subsequent to initial training participation? Excluding compliance requirements, there are many reasons why trainees might need retraining. Perhaps they did not achieve the expected competency levels the first time around. Maybe it's been a while since they participated in their last training program, so their knowledge, skill, attitudes, and/or behavior have eroded or need updating.

Organizations that retrain employees after an initial training experience generally have the advantage of elevating trainee knowledge and skill before a problem surfaces. Training often appears to be recommended as an outcome of an unfortunate work-related event such as formal counseling, a work-site accident, or a customer complaint. When organizations have proactively mandated retraining, trainees are more likely to view the retraining experience in a positive way (that is, "The organization cares about my knowledge and skills being current") than if retraining is only indicated as a reaction to a negative event. Retraining reminders can be built into the organization's training tracking system so that employees are automatically informed when a certain amount of time has passed since the initial training experience. Retraining can be recommended when program evaluation findings (learning, behavior, and/or results data) on a trainee indicate that adequate competency was not achieved with the first training experience. From a legal perspective, organizations can demonstrate their sincere desire to improve an employee's job performance by documenting retraining activities.

Organizations that do not retrain employees after an initial training experience are placed in a more reactive mode. They retrain when job performance issues arise or potential damage has already been done in terms of customer dissatisfaction, fellow employee discontent, and/or financial loss. From a legal perspective, it is difficult to defend a circumstance in which a trainee who did not achieve competency when first trained is allowed to continue to perform job duties without an attempt to retrain and elevate knowledge and skill levels. The organization appears to be negligent in allowing a less-than-competent employee to perform job duties without mandated retraining.

THE AUDIT CONDUCTOR

The training professional can conduct training audits. Doing so on a regular basis can serve as the basis of a performance evaluation goal, along with developing and executing an action plan for rectifying deficiencies uncovered in the audit.

Sometimes, to alleviate any appearance of a conflict of interest, another internal person familiar with the training effort can administer the audit. Another option is for a member of the management team to work in conjunction with the training professional to conduct the training audit and then report their findings and recommended action plans to the appropriate decision-making body for permission to proceed.

Expert external consultants can also administer training audits. Local chapters of professional training and development organizations can provide lists of qualified individuals to undertake the task.

CAPTURING AUDIT RESULTS

The audit conductor can use the form in Exhibit 9.1 to capture and summarize audit results.

Exhibit 9.1. Training Self-Audit

A training audit's purpose is to assess training practices and processes and, where necessary, develop action plans and implement changes to ensure that effective training will be an ongoing activity. Seven key areas are listed below. Please circle "yes" or "no" in answer to each question.

1. Training Needs Identification   **YES**   **NO**

Does the organization have and regularly use a systematic, ongoing training needs assessment process, using either a task analysis or a strategic needs assessment method, to identify specific knowledge, skills, attitudes, and/or behaviors needing improvement?

Comments/Suggested Action Items:

_____

_____

2. Interactive Training   **YES**   **NO**

Does training engage the adult learner interactively, whether in an instructor-led classroom environment, self-paced, or blended training delivery, so that knowledge, skills, attitudes, and behavioral change has a greater opportunity to occur?

Comments/Suggested Action Items:

_____

_____

3. Qualified Trainers and Content Providers   **YES**   **NO**

Whether performed by in-house training staff, internal subject matter experts, or external content providers and/or trainers, has a training professional reviewed and approved the qualifications and training materials of all providers to ensure that they will produce a high quality training experience?

Comments/Action Items:

_____

_____

(*Continued*)

Exhibit 9.1. (*Continued*)

4. Demonstrated Management Support   YES   NO

Is management clearly committed to supporting the training effort? Is there clear evidence that reinforces this assumption?
  Comments/Action Items:

_____

_____

5. Evaluation Processes   YES   NO

Are evaluation processes in place and consistently used? Is action taken once evaluation data is collected and analyzed?
  Comments/Action Items:

_____

_____

6. Training Database   YES   NO

Does a training database track targeted and actual employee participation in training programs and other vital training information? Are reports generated that communicate actionable information for decision makers, training professionals, and managers?
  Comments/Action Items:

_____

_____

7. Retraining Opportunities   YES   NO

Is employee retraining strongly encouraged and undertaken as needed to ensure trainees possess adequate job knowledge, skill, attitudes, and behavior subsequent to initial training participation?
  Comments/Action Items:

_____

_____

RATIONALE

The goal of a training audit is to initiate a process to examine, analyze, and determine whether the organization's training effort is in proper order. Organizations that can honestly and comfortably answer "yes" to each of the seven audit questions probably have an effective, ongoing training program in place. Questions to which the honest answer is uncertainty or a definitive "no" represent opportunities for the training professional to more closely examine training processes and procedures to see how to improve performance and service to the organization.

Conducting a training audit on a regular basis, much like retraining, allows the organization to continually offer a comprehensive, effective, and efficient training program before problems arise. By proactively examining the training effort and making changes where indicated, the organization ensures that training continues to do its job: to facilitate change in employee knowledge, skill, attitudes, and behavior in order to help the enterprise achieve its purpose.

Summary

1. Presenting recommendations to decision-makers to gain approval to proceed is the first step in rolling out the training program to the organization.

2. Marketing the training program internally to the entire organization allows everyone to become enthused and prepared for the upcoming training programs.

3. Publicizing success to stakeholders builds support for the training effort and justifies the organization's investment.

4. Conducting a regular training audit keeps successful practices in place and mandates changes to those processes that need alteration.

REFERENCES

2005 Industry Report. (2005, December). *Training*, p. 14.

2006 Industry Report. (2006, December). *Training*, p. 21.

2006 Staff Education and Development Catalog. (2006, August). San Diego, CA: University of California San Diego.

2007 Training Top 125. (2007, March). *Training*, p. 58.

2005 Industry Report. (2005, December). *Training*, p. 14.

2006 Industry Report. (2006, December). *Training*, p. 21.

2006 Staff Education and Development Catalog. (2006, August). San Diego, CA: University of California San Diego.

2007 Training Top 125. (2007, March). *Training*, p. 58.

Alliger, G.A. (1997). Meta-analysis of the relations among training criteria. *Personnel Psychology, 41*(1), 63–105.

Analytics: Understanding the Economics of Learning. (2001). Redwood Shores, CA: Saba.

ASTD. (1999). *1999 state of the industry report.* Alexandria, VA: American Society for Training and Development.

ASTD. (2005). *2005 state of the industry report.* Alexandria, VA: American Society for Training and Development.

ASTD. (2006). *2006 state of the industry report.* Alexandria, VA: American Society for Training and Development.

ASTD. (2007). *2007 state of the industry report.* Alexandria, VA: American Society for Training and Development.

Bass, B.M., & Barrett, G.V. (1972). *Man, work and organizations.* Boston, MA: Allyn and Bacon.

Bernthal, P.R., Colteryahn, K., Davis, P., Naughton, J., Rothwell, W.J., & Wellins, R. (2004). *Mapping the future: Shaping new workplace learning and performance competencies.* Alexandria, VA: ASTD Press.

Boehle, S. (2006, August). Are you too nice to train? *Training, 43*(8), 16–22.

Bratton, W. (2003, February). Training the 21st century police officer. Every cop a teacher: A call for creating an effective lessons-learned program. Available: www.rand.org/pubs/monograph_reports/MR1745/MR1745.ch3

Bureau of State Audits. (1999). *California Science Center: It does not ensure fair and equitable treatment of employees, thus exposing the state to risk.* (Report No. 98115.1). Sacramento, CA: California State Auditor.

Caldwell, R.M., & Marcel, M. (1985, January). Evaluating trainers: In search of the perfect method. *Training,* pp. 17–23.

Catalanello, R., & Kirkpatrick, D. (1968, May). Evaluating training programs: The state of the art. *Training and Development Journal,* pp. 2–9.

Clark, R., & Estes, F. (2002). *Turning research into results: A guide to selecting the right performance solutions.* Atlanta, GA: CEP Press.

Collins, J., & Porras, J. (1994). *Built to last: Successful habits of visionary companies.* New York: HarperBusiness.

Collins, J. (2001). *Good to great: Why some companies make the leap . . . and others don't.* New York: HarperBusiness.

Collins, J. (2005, November 28). Lessons from a student of life. *Business Week.*

Deming, W.E. (1982). *Quality, productivity, and competitive position.* Boston, MA: MIT Center of Advanced Engineering.

Drucker, P. (1946). *Concept of the corporation.* Boston, MA: Transaction Publishers.

Drucker, P. (1954). *The practice of management.* New York: Perennial Library.

Drucker, P. (1959). *Landmarks of tomorrow: A report on the new "post-modern" world.* New York: Harper and Brothers.

Drucker, P. (1982). *Age of discontinuity.* New York: Perennial Library.

Equal Employment Opportunity Commission. (2007). *Sexual harassment.* Available: www.eeoc.gov/types/sexual_harassment.html

Gillis, L., & Bailey, A. (2003). The bottom line on ROI: The Jack Phillips approach. *The Canadian Learning Journal,* 7(1), 7–10.

Glaser, R. (1994). *Training needs assessment tool.* King of Prussia, PA: HRDQ.

Harrison, G. (1967). Within you without you. *Sgt. Peppers Lonely Hearts Club Band.* New York: Capital Records.

International Board of Standards for Training, Performance, and Instruction. (2003). *Instructor Competencies Study.* Ann Arbor, MI: IBSTPI.

Jagger, M., & Richards, K. (1969). You can't always get what you want. *Let it bleed.* New York: London Records.

Jones, J.E., & Pfeiffer, J.W. (Eds.) (1979). *The 1979 annual handbook for group facilitators.* San Francisco, CA: Pfeiffer.

Judd, S. (2007, November 13). The skill of training staff. *Evening Gazette* (UK), p. 6.

Kirkpatrick, D. (1975). Techniques for evaluating programs: Parts 1, 2, 3 and 4. *Evaluating Training Programs.* Alexandria, VA: ASTD Press.

Kirkpatrick, D. (1978, September). Evaluating in-house training programs. *Training and Development Journal*, pp. 6–9.

Kirkpatrick, D., & Kirkpatrick, J. (2006). Evaluating training programs: The four levels (3rd ed.). San Francisco, CA: Berrett-Koehler.

Knowles, M. (1980, May). How do you get people to be self-directed learners? *Training and Development Journal*, pp. 96–99.

Kornik, J., & Weinstein, M. (2006, November) Salary survey. *Training*, p. 19.

Lewin, K. (1947, June). Frontiers in group dynamics: Concept, method, and reality in social sciences, social equilibria and social change. *Human Relations, 1*(1), 5–41.

Mager, R.F. (1962). *Preparing instructional objectives.* Belmont, CA. Fearon.

Metzler, C.J. (2003, Spring). Selecting the diversity consultant: Ensuring the emperor has clothes. *Workforce Diversity Reader*, pp. 1–8.

Meyers, S.A. (2005). *Why are we killing ourselves: A look at accidental shootings of police officers by police officers.* Available: www.operationaltactics.com

Mitchell, G. (1987). *The trainer's handbook.* New York: AMACOM.

Moskowitz, M. (2004). *Evaluate your famous employee.* Unpublished training exercise.

Moskowitz, M. (2007). *What have we learned from 314 training needs assessments?* Unpublished research study.

Moskowitz, M. (2007). *The impact of sexual harassment prevention training on trainees' likelihood to ignore harassing behavior.* Unpublished research study.

Phillips, K. (2004). *Performance appraisal skills inventory* (2nd ed.). King of Prussia, PA: HRDQ.

Phillips, J. (2004, December). *The myths and mysteries of ROI.* Presented at an ASTD/SHRM Conference, Los Angeles, California.

Rae, L. (2002). *Assessing the value of your training: The evaluation process from training needs to the board.* Brookfield, VT: Ashgate.

Roberts, B. (2007). Data-driven human capital decisions. *HR Magazine, 52*(3), 105–108.

Smith, M.K. (2002). Malcolm Knowles, informal adult education, self-direction and andragogy. *The encyclopedia of informal education.* www.infed.org/thinkers?et-knowl.htm.

Special Report Series. (2006). EPLI (Employment Practices Liability Insurance): Understanding the Exposure and Preventing Claims. Available: www.employeradvisorsnetwork.com.

Training programme evaluation. (2007, October) Available at: www.businessballs.com/trainingprogramevaluation.htm

Wallace, S.R., & Twichell, C.M. (1953). An evaluation of a training course for life insurance agents. *Personnel Psychology, 6*, 25–43.

Weathersby, R.B. (2005). *Limiting, not creating liability in employment relations training.* Southlake, TX: Employment Practices Solutions.

Wheeler, D. (1992). *Understanding statistical process control.* Knoxville, TN: SPC Press.

Wikipedia. (2007, April). *Kurt Lewin.* Available: http://en.wikipedia.org/wiki/Kurt_Lewin.

Wikipedia. (2007, April). *Truth or consequences.* Available: http://en.wikipedia.org/wiki/Truth_or_Consequences.

Wikipedia. (2007, September). *Peter Drucker.* Available:

Wikipedia. (2007, September). *W. Edwards Deming.* Available: http://en.wikipedia.org/wiki/W._Edwards Deming.

Williams, S.W. (2001, Spring). The effectiveness of subject-matter experts as technical trainers. *Human Resource Development Quarterly,* pp. 91–97

Woodward, N.H. (2007a). Making safety job no.1. *HR Magazine, 52*(1), 60–65.

Woodward, N.H. (2007b). To make changes, manage them. *HR Magazine, 52*(5), 63–67.

INDEX

About the Author

Since 1978, **Michael Moskowitz** has been a human resource and training professional.

As the owner/founder of Training Q and A Consulting, Michael's client list includes Kaiser Permanente, AT&T, Buck Knives, Dimension One Spas, Scripps Research Institute, Sanyo North America, Chicano Federation, Unisys Corporation, American Tower Corporation, Bidland Systems, CliniComp Corporation, Elemental Software, Gafcon, Inc., Getchell Construction, Hurkes Design Associates, Impact Solutions, Inc., Oridean, Inc., Physician Management Resources, Inc., RD Instruments, Signal Pharmaceutical, Tachyon, Inc., TruSolutions Computers, Leucadia Electric, and Underwater Kinetics, Inc.

His previous work experience includes HR manager, Next-Wave Telecom; HR manager, AirTouch Cellular; HR director, Sharp Cabrillo Hospital; training and employee relations director, Mercy Hospital and Medical Center; staff education and development manager, University of California San Diego; and personnel development specialist, Kaiser Permanente Medical Care Program.

Michael was an instructor at California State University San Marcos, teaching HR management in the College of Business Administration. Michael was on the faculty at the University of Phoenix, where he taught personnel management in the School of Human Resources. He is an instructor at the University of California San Diego Extension, teaching training and development in the Business and Management Program.

Michael holds an M.A. degree in psychology from United States International University and a B.A. degree in psychology from Queens College, City University of New York.

Michael is married with two children and lives in Oceanside, California.

What will you find on pfeiffer.com?

- The best in workplace performance solutions for training and HR professionals

- Downloadable training tools, exercises, and content

- Web-exclusive offers

- Training tips, articles, and news

- Seamless on-line ordering

- Author guidelines, information on becoming a Pfeiffer Affiliate, and much more

Discover more at www.pfeiffer.com